Economics as a Science

ECONOMICS
AS A
SCIENCE

Kenneth E. Boulding

Professor of Economics
Institute of Behavioral Science
University of Colorado

McGraw-Hill Book Company

New York   St. Louis   San Francisco
London   Sydney   Toronto   Mexico   Panama

Economics as a Science

Library of Congress Catalog Card Number 75-105420

1234567890   VBVB   79876543210

This book was set in Janson by
Vail-Ballou Press, Inc., and printed on
permanent paper and bound by Vail-Ballou
Press, Inc. The designer was Paula Tuerk;
the drawings were done by BMA Associates, Inc.
The editor was Cynthia Newby. Paul B. Poss
supervised the production.

PREFACE

The first four of these essays originated in a seminar which I gave in the summer of 1968 at the University of Colorado to a group of teachers, most of them from high schools, in an experienced-teacher program. The fifth, sixth, and seventh essays were added subsequently, the sixth essay being a slightly revised version of my Presidential Address to the American Economic Association in December, 1968.

The main purpose of these essays is to introduce those who already have some acquaintance with economics to what might be called the larger scientific background of the subject. The seminar out of which these essays grew was motivated by the feeling that, especially for those who were going back to teach economics in the schools, a feeling for the significance and the background of the discipline was even more important than the acquisition of specific analytical techniques. The trees of the economic forest are so intriguing that it is all too easy not see the wood. These essays are intended to give the reader not only a certain feeling for the little wood that is economics but for the larger landscape in which the wood is set.

Nobody will become an economist merely by reading these essays.

I hope, however, that those who are already economists may get a broader perspective on what they are and where they stand, and those who are not economists may get at least a tourist's eye view of what is perhaps not just a wood, but a very productive orchard.

I would like to thank the teachers who participated in the seminar and who gave many helpful and interesting suggestions. I would like to thank Dr. Irving Morrissett and the staff of the Social Science Education Consortium at Boulder, who organized the seminar and helped in the preparation of the manuscript. I would also like to thank my secretary, Mrs. Vivian Wilson, for her unfailing and cheerful assistance on this and many other projects.

Kenneth E. Boulding

CONTENTS

ONE

Economics as a Social Science

The total social system consists of all the people in the world, all the roles which they occupy, all their patterns of behavior, all their inputs and outputs which are relevant to other human beings, and all the organizations and groups that they belong to. This is, of course, a very large, complicated system. Nevertheless, it is convenient to separate it from other systems of the world even though all the world's systems interact and form a total system of the planet. Just as geologists and oceanographers study the lithosphere and the hydrosphere, meteorologists study the atmosphere, and biologists study the biosphere, so we may say that social scientists study the sociosphere, which operates as a system at a somewhat different level of organization from the others.

In the study of the rocks of the lithosphere we can confine ourselves for the most part within a fairly simple physical, chemical, and mechanical system, although there is an interface with the biosphere in the creation of soil and with the sociosphere in mining, dam building, flood control, and so on. Similarly, the atmosphere can be studied as a very homogeneous, mainly physical, system, although here again when we consider its chemical composition, the interaction with the biosphere through respiration and with the sociosphere through pollution cannot be neglected. A study of the biosphere introduces the interaction of populations through ecology and the perpetuation and evolution of patterns of life through genetic change, which represents a systems level beyond that of the lithosphere. Similarly the sociosphere represents a systems level beyond the biosphere. It includes such things as knowledge, complex images, especially images of the future, self-consciousness, symbolic systems, and so on, which either are not found or are found only at a very primitive level in the biosphere.

Every system has two aspects—its "state description" on the one hand and its "dynamics" on the other. The state description is what the term implies—it is a description of the state of the system as of a moment of time. Such a description has to be abstract in the sense that we would be quite incapable of producing in language of any kind a full description of the state of even quite simple systems. A great descriptive writer like James Joyce can spend a whole novel describing the events in the mind of a single person for a single night; to do this he has to strain the resources of the English language to the breaking point and even then he cannot encompass more than a fraction of the reality. The description of the enormous complexity of the sociosphere even at a single moment in time must involve abstraction to an extreme degree. It is the principle business of the social sciences, indeed, to develop those abstractions which are most useful and which give us the most significant information. It is a very fundamental principle indeed that knowledge is always gained by the orderly loss of information, that is, by condensing and abstracting and indexing the great buzzing confusion of information that comes from the world around us into a form which we can appreciate and comprehend.

The dynamics of the system consist of a succession of state descriptions and the perception of the patterns in this succession. We have to think of the real world as a four-dimensional continuum in three dimensions of space and one of time. Dynamics, therefore, consist simply of a state description of the system in these four dimensions. The importance of dynamics is that it is only through the perception of the patterns in the space-time continuum that we can form images of the future, and it is images of the future which determine present behavior through the process of decision; the alternative choices that we decide among are all alternative images of the future. We obviously cannot make decisions about the past, although we can change our images of it. Thus, we are able to find our way around town because we have an image of the future in which the physical space around us—the streets, the buildings, and so on—has a high degree of stability. We expect the town tomorrow to be very much what it is today, apart from a few minor changes. We plan our lives in regard to jobs, education, insurance, marriage, family, and so on because we become aware from the observation of other lives that individual human life follows a certain rather small repertoire of patterns. We perceive that all age in much the same way and are all subject to accidents. We learn that certain jobs are blind alleys, whereas others lead to advancement. We also learn from memories and records of the past that there are certain great cyclic processes—the succession of day and night and the seasons, the great clockwork movements of celestial mechanics—and we are able to project these processes into the future.

Simple dynamic systems, such as the solar system, may be called "difference systems" because they can be described mathematically by difference or differential equations. If, for instance, in any system the difference between today and tomorrow is stable and can be described by a stable function, then if we know the state of the system today we can predict it tomorrow; knowing it tomorrow we can predict it the next day, knowing it the next day we can predict it the day after, and so on indefinitely into the future. This would be a difference system of the first degree. If there is a stable relationship between the state of the system tomorrow and the state today and the state yesterday, we would have a difference system of the second degree. Almost all of celestial mechanics can be described in terms of systems as simple as this.

Difference systems are highly characteristic of what might be called mechanical systems, though they are sometimes useful as first approximations in both biological and social systems. In biological systems there are two typical dynamic patterns. One is the "creode," the pattern of development of the single living organism from the fertilized egg to its final death and dissolution. The other is the "phylum," the great evolutionary tree which results from inheritance and the mutation-selection process. We are familiar with the concept of the creode in the pattern of human life from conception to death, as it is determined in large part by the genetic information contained in the fertilized egg. It is this that determines the biological growth of the body through childhood into maturity and its final decay into old age and death. Up to now there has been very little that we have been able to do about this process. Up to now, at any rate, no man by taking thought has been able to add a cubit to his stature or postpone the process of aging.

The evolutionary process rests first on the fact that in any given physical environment a given "gene pool" will result in an ecological equilibrium of interacting populations of species. Evolution is the process by which an ecological equilibrium is continually disturbed by mutations in the gene pool itself and changes in the conditions of equilibrium that result from changes in the physical environment.

A useful analytical device for the study of systems of all kinds is the concept of equilibrium. An equilibrium system is one in which the state of the system tomorrow is the same as it is today. There are many kinds of equilibrium. The simplest is mechanical equilibrium such as that of a book resting on a table. Here the position of the book, if nobody moves it, will be the same tomorrow as it is today, simply because the resultant of all the forces acting on the book is zero, the forces which make for change in one direction being exactly balanced by resistances which prevent such a change. A more complex form of equilibrium, important in both biological and social systems, is homeostasis or cybernetic equilibrium. This is the type of equilibrium which characterizes what are called "open systems," that is, systems which maintain a structure in the midst of some kind of a throughput of materials or other "role occupants." One of the simplest open systems is the flame, which maintains a constant structure of chemical composition in its different parts because it is able to maintain a continual throughput, with an input of combustible materials on the bottom and an output of burnt gases at the top. Every living organism has this flamelike characteristic, as poets have often noted. Every living organism maintains a certain physical structure in the middle of a throughput of materials, breathing in and eating, just as the flame feeds on its combustible material, and breathing out or excreting, just as the flame gives off its burned gases. The chemical process of oxidation indeed which gives heat to the flame also gives heat to the living organism. A social organization likewise is an open system and must maintain an equilibrium of this kind. Thus, a university is continually taking in freshmen and turning them in successive time zones into sophomores, juniors, and seniors and excreting them as alumni.

There is an important difference between what may be called defenseless open systems like the flame—a river and the soil [1] would be

[1] Every segment of a river and every zone in the soil receives material from the segment or zone before it and delivers material to the one after it.

other good examples—and defended open systems and that is that the latter are capable of search and can process information into images of the world around it. This perhaps is one of the most fundamental differences between living and nonliving organizations. When the candle is exhausted, the flame does not flit around the room looking for another candle. It simply goes out. If an amoeba cannot find food in its present environment, it will move and will go around looking for food. It can differentiate between food and nonfood and when it meets food it ingests it. The higher we go in the sphere of life, the more complicated does the search and information process become. We can see this illustrated in the various mechanisms which are used to maintain constancy of temperature. A flame which is cooled too much by blowing will simply go out. It has no defense at all against temperature change. Simple one-celled organisms will move to the most comfortable part of the environment. They have very little in the way of internal defense against external temperature change. Reptiles are not much better, though they will move into the sun. The development of the so-called warm-blooded animals was a great step forward in evolution because it meant that there were organisms with internal defenses against temperature change. Warm-blooded animals have a cybernetic mechanism like the thermostat; if the outside environment cools down below the optimum level, they will burn fuel faster or take shelter. When we come to man we see an enormous repertoire of defenses against adverse outside temperatures, including purely biological ones like teeth chattering, pores closing and opening, changes in metabolism, and so on. On the other hand, man has also developed social defenses such as houses, fires, central heating, clothing, air conditioning, and so on to keep himself at the optimum temperature for biological and social activity. Nowadays his very artifacts are in a sense "warm-blooded," for the internal temperature of the average house is regulated by its own cybernetic apparatus. Even the automobile is a warm-blooded or at least a warm-aired creature, maintaining a constant inside temperature in the face of wide external temperature changes.

Social organizations, likewise, build defenses against external changes. In a college, for instance, the admissions office sees to it that there is a constant stream of entering freshmen every year. The deans and executive committees keep a watchful eye on departments that may decay and are careful to replace professors, as they retire or leave, with adequate substitutes. The trustees or regents replace the president when necessary and keep a watchful eye on the administration, and occasionally even on the faculty. The trustees may be self-perpetuating or they may in turn be subject to replacement, for instance, by the people of the state. All this involves what might be called defensive machinery, since it is designed to maintain the structure of an organization in the face of random changes in the environment.

As the social system, or sociosphere, is the most complex of all our systems, it is not surprising to find eventually a whole repertoire of analytical devices used in the investigation of its state description and its dynamics. Even systems as simple as difference systems have some value though they do not carry us very far. Thus, we often project trends in social systems assuming, for instance, stable rates of change or growth. We may be more sophisticated and assume changing rates of growth—supposing, for instance, that the rate of growth of a system will decline as the system gets larger, thus producing the familiar logistic or ogive [2] pattern of a growth process. A good deal

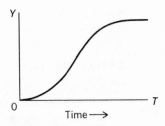

FIGURE 1-1

[2] An ogive curve is one in which the rate of growth continually diminishes as growth proceeds, as in the figure; time is measured horizontally and Y—the quantity that is growing—is measured vertically.

of time has been spent, by economists especially, in trying to develop mechanical models of the business cycle, somewhat along the lines of celestial mechanics. On the whole, these have been a failure, mainly because the business cycle itself is a very irregular phenomenon with strong random elements in it and thus does not conform to the patterns of simple difference systems.

The concept of the creode also has some use in analyzing social systems, though biological analogies have to be used with great care. There is, however, some similarity between the origin and rise of a social organization such as a firm, a church, a state, or a university and the kind of processes which go on in biological organisms. A social organization always originates as an information structure of some kind, usually in the mind of its founder or founders, which has some analogies to the gene. Likewise its development is the result of a built-in code, expressed in constitutions, charters, laws, bylaws, organization charts, plans, and the like, which is modified by a constant input and output of information as the organization gets older. But whereas eventual aging and death is coded into the genetic structure of all complex biological organizations, this is not necessarily true in the case of social organizations, the latter being, theoretically at least, capable of almost continual self-renewal. There may be some social organizations such as terminable foundations, which have their dissolution written into their original charters. Most social organizations, however, are "genetically" immortal and die only as a result of adverse external circumstances, such as the bankruptcy of a firm or the conquest of a state, to which their defensive machinery is inadequate to respond. The family is a curious example of a social organization with an amoeba type of quasi-death by fission as children grow up and marry and establish families of their own; therefore, it does not have the same kind of role-maintaining apparatus as, shall we say, the corporation or the church.

There are some striking parallels in the social system to the distinction which is so important in biological systems between the genotype and the phenotype, the genotype being the genetic code in the fertilized egg which organizes the growth and development of the phenotype—the living animal. In the social system what one has to look for are genotypical relationships which have the power of creating a process of development of social organization and role structure. An organization is primarily a structure of roles; its personnel function essentially as role occupants. A role indeed is a "hole" or a position in the structure of inputs and outputs of all kinds of commodities and communications. It may be thought of as a "node" in the input-output network insofar as it receives inputs and gives off outputs. A role, however, may be occupied by a variety of persons; it may even be occupied by a machine. When we look for the genotypes in social systems, therefore, what we are looking for are role-creating relationships. I have distinguished three broad classes of such relationships—threat, exchange, and integrative relationships. A threat relationship originates when one person says to another, "You do something that I want (that is, occupy a certain role) or I will do something that you do not want." If the threatened person submits, we get a threat-submission system which can be fairly powerful in creating roles. The threatener of course must have credibility, that is, the threatened person must believe that if he does not perform the imposed role he will in fact have something done to him that he does not like, "something" being the equivalent of a production of "bads." A rather surprising phenomenon is the extent to which spiritual threat systems imposed by priesthoods have persisted for many generations without any demonstrated ability to carry out their implied threats. A material threat system, however, imposed by a political organization such as a monarchy seems to need a certain amount of capability in the shape of police or an army, and frequently has to restore the credibility of its threats by actually carrying them out.

Exchange develops when somebody says to somebody else, "You do something that I want and I'll do something that you want." This is the most generalized form of the exchange relationship which may therefore take the form of simply occupying mutually agreeable roles. A commodity exchange is an important variant or rather subset of the generalized exchange relationship in which A says to B, "I will give you something that you want if you will give me something that I want." A commodity exchange however tends to produce role development because it induces specialization. People discover that where exchange opportunities are continually available, it pays them to specialize in the production of one commodity which they can exchange for others which are similarly produced by specialized producers. This is the famous principle of the division of labor as developed so eloquently by Adam Smith. Exchange, therefore, turns out to be a very powerful organizer with much more evolutionary potential than threat. The threat system can develop slavery and classical civilization. The latter, however, has a very limited horizon of development, and the breakthrough into the modern developmental process of the last three hundred years unquestionably could not have taken place except in a society in which exchange had developed to the point where it predominated. This, of course, is the historical significance of capitalism, which is precisely a society in which exchange has become a more important source of power than threat.

The third social genotype is a little harder to identify clearly and it includes indeed a great variety of relationships. There are, however, relationships, which cannot be described under the headings of threat and exchange, which involve primarily the mutual acceptance of status as a role-creating factor. I have called these "integrative relationships." The mutual acceptance of status as a role-creating factor unquestionably begins in the family where the sheer biology of the situation creates a status superiority of the parents over the children. An integrative relationship then takes form when somebody says to somebody else, "You do something because of what you are and what I am." It is integrative relationships then that create such things as community, personal identity, internalized role motivations, the legitimization of authority, and so on. Without integrative relationships indeed neither threat nor exchange can maintain a continuing relationship and organization. Both threat and exchange relationships must be legitimated if they are to be continuously capable of creating roles.

With this social genetic structure in mind let us now take a look at the various segments of the sociosphere to see how they relate to each other and to this scheme of social genetics. We may form several divisions, the first being the economy or the econosphere. This consists primarily of that segment of the sociosphere which is organized through exchange and especially commodity exchange. We visualize each individual as a node in a vast network of inputs and outputs of exchangeables, which include both goods and services. In any complicated system there has to be a medium of exchange, which is almost always money, so that the distribution of stocks of money and the input and output of money flows are an important part of the econosphere. The economy is likewise concerned with production, that is, the transformation of various kinds of inputs, such as labor and materials, into exchangeable outputs of product.

The economy also includes a financial system which consists essentially of the distribution and relation of balance sheet items, including debt, securities, real capital, and net worth. The production, exchange, and financial systems are, of course, all closely interrelated. Indeed it is hard to imagine any event which does not affect all three.

Included in, or at least very intimately related to, the economy is what may be called the "grants economy," that is, the network of one-way transfers of exchangeables throughout the world. An exchange is a two-way transfer of exchangeables—A gives something to B and B gives something to A. A grant is a one-way transfer of exchangeables in which A gives something to B but B does not give anything in the way of an exchangeable, at least, to A. The grants economy in turn may be divided into the private grants economy, which includes such things as charitable donations and foundation grants, and the public grants economy, which includes a large part of taxation and government expenditure.

One typical institution of the economy is the firm, which is concerned primarily with the transformation of inputs of exchangeables into outputs of exchangeables. In the modern world the most common form of the firm is the corporation, though partnerships and sole proprietorships continue to exist. The banking and the financial systems, the stock market, and the foreign exchange markets are also characteristic institutions of the economy and are the main institutional representatives of the financial system. Governments also have very important economic aspects. In socialist countries, of course, the government economy is dominant, and the society is something like a one-firm state in which the government or its agencies purchase most of the inputs and produce most of the outputs. Even in market-oriented societies the government is usually by far and away the largest economic organization and tends to account for roughly a quarter of the total economy. All social organizations have economic aspects, for none of them can survive without inputs and outputs of exchangeables. Thus the family is an important economic unit, so is the church, so are schools and universities, hospitals, and other institutions that we do not think of primarily as economic.

While the economy is naturally dominated by exchange and exchangeables it must not be thought that it is independent of the other social organizers. In the background, for instance, lies the threat system which is implied in the legal order. Unless there is reasonable security of property and enforcement of contracts, an economic system cannot reach any degree of complexity. On the other side, it also depends very strongly on certain integrative relationships. Unless, for instance, there is a wide degree of trust and honesty, any complex financial institution, such as banking, the credit card, or, in fact, credit in general, could not develop beyond rather a primitive form. The degree of mutual trust indeed which is involved in a complex financial system is quite extraordinary, and the failure of the integrative system of a country to develop concepts of mutuality, trust, and community beyond the confines of the family or the small intimate group is often one of the major obstacles to its economic development.

Another very important segment of the sociosphere is the "polity," that aspect of the sociosphere which deals primarily with organizations exercising threat. This entity may be divided roughly into the domestic polity and the international polity—the domestic polity being enshrined in organizations such as national governments, parliaments, bureaucracies, civil services, state and local governments, school boards, water boards, and all the innumerable fauna of the political system which characteristically depend not on uncoerced exchange but on some exercise of police power. For instance, in the tax system exchangeables flow toward the organization with tax power, not because their producers expect them to be exchanged directly for products which the organization produces, but because they know that if they do not make these transfers they will be subject to penalties. Domestic polities are characterized on the whole by what might be called legitimated threat, especially by legitimated threat-submission systems. We submit to paying our taxes, we submit to being drafted, which is a form of taxation in kind, we submit to all sorts of traffic regulations and legal codes as individuals because if we do not submit we will be penalized and we regard submission as preferable to defiance. This submission, especially in democratic societies, is legitimated by a political apparatus of constitutions, elections, parliaments, and so on, which implies that we set up organizations to coerce ourselves. There is a real difference between those polities which are tyrannical in the sense that the threats are not self-imposed but imposed from outside and those polities which are democratic or constitutional in the sense that there is machinery for changing the threats if people begin to feel that they are illegitimate. Thus, the more a polity is based on a self-legitimated system the closer it comes to constitutionality and democracy.

Whereas the domestic polity is characterized mainly by legitimated threat-submission, the international polity is characterized mainly by deterrence, that is, a threat-counterthreat system. There are four major possible reactions to an initial threat: submission, defiance, flight, or counterthreat. A threat-counterthreat system is one in which A says to B, "You do something that I want, or I'll do something that you don't want," and B replies by saying, "If you do something that *I* don't want, I'll do something that *you* don't want." Deterrence systems unfortunately are apt to be unstable, for a very good reason; if the probability of the threats being carried out were zero, they would obviously fail to deter. If, however, the probability of the threats being carried out is positive, then every so often such an event will occur. This is why the international system is continually breaking down into war. Stable deterrence indeed is a myth in which we seem to have some faith in this country. We are likely to have that trust rudely shattered.

Just as the economy must include certain elements from the threat and the integrative systems, so the polity must include certain elements of exchange and have strong integrative relationships or it cannot organize permanent structures. Illegitimate threat (the bandit) can organise temporary relationships, but threat must be legitimated if it is to create a permanent organization. Exchange creeps into the polity when the government starts to be productive instead of merely exploitative, that is, when people begin to feel that they get something for their taxes. Similarly, in the international polity exchange creeps in through the practice of diplomacy and bargaining. Exchange here is not always an exchange of commodities; it may be an exchange of "postures." Then, of course, occasionally diplomatic bargaining includes things like foreign aid and the transfer of territories which fall very much within the scope of the economy.

The other segments of the social system are not perhaps so clearly defined as the economy and the polity, but we can certainly distinguish a segment for which it is hard to find a name but which is concerned with learning, knowledge, and information flows. Thus, just as in the economy we regard each individual or economic organization as a node in a network of inputs and outputs of commodities and exchangeables so we can conceive each individual or group of individuals as a node in a global network of inputs and outputs of information, symbols, and language. This concept is particularly important because it is the "infosphere," to coin a name for it, which is the prime creator of "human nature" and the nature of human organizations such as nations, corporations, and churches. Biologically, the human organism is endowed at birth with enormous potential for receiving and processing information but with extremely little informational content. Whereas the lower animals tend to get most of their informational content from their genetic structures as the latter build up their nervous systems, in the case of the human animal the specific genetic component consists almost entirely of potential rather than content. It is hardly an exaggeration to say, therefore, that there is no such thing as innate human nature, or at least that what is created by the genes consists mainly of an enormous diversity of potential. What the individual human being becomes, therefore, depends mainly on the information inputs, outputs, and feedbacks to which he has been exposed since infancy, even though these are not unrelated to his biological constitution and appearance. Thus, a black child growing up in the United States will receive certain inputs of information which are a function of the fact that he looks black and these will affect the ultimate content of his nervous system, but the results, whatever they are, will be determined much more by information inputs from outside, than by information contained in his genes.

The infosphere then consists of inputs and outputs of conversation, books, television, radio, speeches, church services, classes, and lectures as well as information received from the physical world by personal observation. We have not been able to reduce the infosphere to anything like the abstract order that we have achieved in the economy or even the polity. Nevertheless, it is clearly a segment of the sociosphere in its own right, and indeed it has considerable claim to dominate the other segments. It can be argued that development of any kind is essentially a learning process and that it is primarily dependent on a network of information flows. Just as the economy and polity have institutions which are peculiarly associated with them, so there are institutions which are peculiarly characteristic of the infosphere. Among these is the family, within the communication network of which the child grows up. It is the family that determines the native language and what might be called the native culture which surrounds him. As the child matures, however, other institutions—the church, the school, the newspaper, the radio, the television, the book, and so on—tend to take over.

One of the problems of the description of the infosphere is that there is no easily definable unit of socially significant information comparable to, for instance, the monetary unit in the economy, or even the vote in the polity. We have, of course, a unit of information in the "bit," which is valuable in defining certain quantitative aspects of the infosphere, but we have to recognize also that a conversation of the president of the United States on the hot line to the Soviet Union in a crisis has more significance than the conversation of a teenager, even though it may contain the same number of bits of information and from the point of view of the telephone company be identical with the latter. The key problem here is that the dynamics of the social system are dominated by the growth of knowledge, and knowledge is not a simple one-dimensional additive quantity. In the case of the economy, it is not unreasonable to suppose that the increase in the stock of something in any particular location in a given period is equal to the input of it minus the output. This is what I have sometimes called the "bathtub theorem"; the rate at which the stock of water in a bathtub is increasing is the difference between the rate at which it is flowing in and the rate at which it is flowing out. In the case of the infosphere unfortunately the bathtub theorem does not apply. Knowledge is not the difference between the information input and the information output, even though they are certainly related. An individual who had no information input would not know anything; similarly, the more input an individual has received, the more knowledge he may be expected to have. On the other hand, the relationship is certainly not a simple linear one. We have to face the problem also of negative knowledge, that is, knowing things that are not so. A great deal of input of information creates negative knowledge, as we pick up the superstitions of the culture around us.

A very important aspect of the infosphere is the learning of values and preferences and ethical systems. The genetic basis of values in human organisms is very primitive and consists of little more than an innate liking for milk and mother and a moderate dislike of being wet and hearing loud noises. All our other values and preferences are added on to this through our information inputs. We cannot assume, therefore, that preferences are given—a fact, incidentally, which destroys a great deal of what is called welfare economics. The problem of how preferences and ethical systems are learned is not well understood. Ethical systems are, however, the basis of culture, and indeed a culture can almost be defined as a group of people sharing a common ethical system.

We may now ask, "What is the role of the economy in this total social system, which is so sketchily described?" I shall venture to define the economy in a way that is perhaps a little unusual or at least does not correspond to many textbook descriptions. I define the economy as that segment of the total social system which deals primarily with exchange and the institutions of exchange and, by extension, with exchangeables or the goods and services which participate in exchange. I have not defined the economy as that segment of the social system which is concerned with the allocation of scarce resources, which is a frequent definition. Scarce resources may be allocated in many ways other than through exchange. They may be allocated, for instance, through threat, or through the development of integrative relationships. The allocation of scarce resources indeed I have regarded as a property of the total social system, not to be confined to the economy. Thus, in a slave society resources are allocated by the threat capability of the slaveholder, the slave taking a bare minimum subsistence and the slaveholder taking the rest. Similarly, in a family resources are allocated according to the principle of total family responsibility. For instance, a family will often make great sacrifices to send a bright child to college. Here resources are reallocated by the integrative system, rather than by the exchange system.

Similarly, I do not regard the economy as being bounded primarily by the activities of production and consumption of exchangeables, even though these activities are clearly relevant. The economy, that is to say, is not primarily concerned with material provisions, even though they are an important aspect of it. There are certain physical inputs—food, water, air, and protection against the elements —which are essential elements in human survival. The physiological requirements of the human organism impose limits on the social system at this point. Therefore, a social system which does not provide these essential provisions will very soon disappear through the death of its members. Provision, again, however, is an aspect of the total social system, not of the economy itself, and it can take place through habit, custom, threat, and so forth, as well as by an outside system of exchange. Robinson Crusoe, for instance, was concerned with provisions; he was also concerned with the allocation of his scarce resources. Until his man Friday appeared, however, he did not have any exchange with any other persons, although there is a sense in which he had exchanges with his environment. He did not have to worry about any of the usual institutions of economic life. His island had no money, no banking, no trade, no employment, no jobs, no taxes, none of the things in fact which are normally studied in textbooks of economics. Nevertheless the Crusoe economy—one might better say the Crusoe social system—is an interesting starting point for a discussion of comparative social systems.

Simply because the economist is so deeply involved in exchange, he has a peculiar responsibility to call attention to a certain aspect of the social system which is especially characteristic of exchange and is impressed on virtually all social relationships. This is the aspect which can be described as the "terms of trade," even though this is not a very good name for the concept. Every human being, every cluster or organization within the social system, has inputs from and outputs to the rest of the social system. The ratio of inputs to outputs is an important quantity in understanding the behavior of any individual or group. It is this ratio which the "terms of trade" is trying to measure. If our terms of trade are "good," this means that we get a lot of input per unit of what we put out. When the inputs and outputs are heterogeneous aggregates of all sorts of things, as they usually are, the problem of measurement of necessity involves valuation, although the concept of improvement or worsening in the terms of trade does not necessarily depend on exact valuation. Thus, suppose we compare two situations, the first being one in which we put out a certain aggregrate of output and receive a certain aggregate of input, and the second being one in which the aggregate of output is the same but the aggregate of input has been increased by one valuable item. Clearly there has been an improvement in our terms of trade. Where, however, the composition of the aggregate changes, it must be possible to reduce the collection to a single number by a "measure of value." Money is the commonest such measure, and ordinarily, if the aggregate money value of all inputs increases more than the value of all money outputs, we say there has been an improvement in the terms of trade. The terms of trade measure, as you may have noticed, is quite closely related to that of efficiency, which is the ratio of some kind of significant output and some kind of significant input for either a machine or a total organization. The terms of trade of an individual or group represent, as it were, the efficiency of the relevant environment so that the input of the recipient is the output of the environment and the output of the recipient is the input of the environment. This is illustrated in Figure 1-2. The terms of trade of the organism are (B/A).

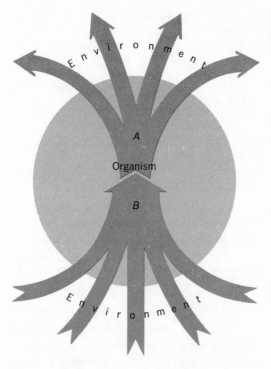

A = Output of organism, input of environment
B = Input of organism, output of environment

FIGURE 1-2

In a simple exchange, of course, the terms of trade are measured by the ratio of exchange, that is, the ratio of what each party gives to what each party gets. If money is one of the things exchanged, the ratio of the exchange then becomes a price. In all relationships, however, where inputs and outputs are involved there is some concept of the terms of trade. In the family, for instance, each member feels that he is giving up something to the family and getting something from the family. If any member feels that his terms of trade fall below a certain critical level, if he feels for instance that he is giving up too much and not getting enough, then there will be a certain amount of strain on the whole performance of the role. If the strain is too big, the family will break up, either through divorce, or through the children running away from home, or something like that. Similarly, in the case of the state, the citizen has a certain terms of trade ratio with his government. He gives something to it and he gets something from it. If he feels his terms of trade are too unfavorable, he will eventually withdraw the consent which he gives to being governed; the result may be some sort of revolution or political overturn or, in a democracy, the election of a new government. The total structure of the terms of trade, therefore, is of enormous importance in explaining the behavior of all persons and organizations in the social system. This is something which economists have studied more than anybody else. The economic concept of a "supply price," for instance, can very easily be generalized to the total social system. This is the concept that holds that the amount of performance is related to the terms of trade which the performance produces and that below a certain level of terms of trade the performance will eventually stop. Thus the concept of what might be called the generalized price structure, that is, the total structure of all terms of trade, is of enormous importance in determining the dynamics of performance in the total social system. This is perhaps the major contribution of economics to the total study of society even though not all economists would recognize it as such.

Another important contribution of economics to the total study of society is in the field of decision theory, which is the study of how performance reacts to perceived changes in the environment of the actor. This, however, will be the subject of another chapter.

TWO

Economics as an Ecological Science

Ecology is a term used in the biological sciences to describe a total system of interrelated populations of different species. Such a system of interrelated populations is called an ecosystem. Even though, strictly speaking, the world is a single ecosystem, it can be divided into "habitats" such as a prairie field, an arctic tundra, a tropical forest, a desert, the Arctic Ocean, and so on. A habitat is characterized by relative uniformity of physical environment and fairly close interaction of all the biological species involved.

The concept is clearly extensible to social systems, which also consist of interacting populations of many different kinds. The human population itself can be divided into many different social species—occupational groups, religious groups, national groups, linguistic groups, cultural groups, and the like. The social system likewise includes populations of human artifacts such as automobiles, houses, machines, and so on and populations of domestic animals and vegetables, which are in part human artifacts. The system consists also of populations of organizations—trade unions, churches, counties, states, banks, steel corporations, and so on. All these populations continually interact with each other.

The first principle of an ecosystem is that everything depends on everything else, and the first theorem is that if everything depends on everything else, an ecological equilibrium may be possible. More specifically, in a closed ecosystem, or habitat, each species will have an equilibrium population size which will depend upon the population sizes of all the other species, including nonbiological species and populations such as quantities of minerals, chemicals, and so on. Here we expand the concept of a population to mean anything which can be more or less. Thus, the equilibrium population size of a living species such as rabbits will be larger, the larger the population of the things that it eats, and smaller, the larger the population of the things that eat it, or in general will be larger, the larger the population of things in the environment that are friendly to it and smaller, the larger the population of things in the environment that are hostile to it. What is meant by an equilibrium of a total system is that set of sizes of populations of all its constituents which is consistent in the sense that each species finds that the level of population size of all other species is such that its own population will neither increase nor decrease.

We can express this mathematically by supposing first that we have an ecosystem with n populations with sizes $x_1, x_2, \ldots, x_n$. Then for any population x_i we postulate a partial equilibrium function which can be written

$$x_i = F_i (x_1, x_2, \ldots, x_{i-1}, x_{i+1}, \ldots, x_n)$$

This simply states mathematically what we said above, that given the sizes of all populations except one there will be a unique equilibrium size of the excepted population. As we can write an equation of this kind for each population, this gives us n equations and n unknowns as follows:

$$x_1 = F_1 \ (x_2, x_3, \ldots , x_n)$$
$$x_2 = F_2 \ (x_1, x_3, \ldots , x_n)$$
$$\ldots \ldots \ldots \ldots \ldots \ldots \ldots \quad (1)$$
$$x_n = F_n \ (x_1, x_2, \ldots , x_{n-1})$$

It is a well-known algebraic theorem that where we have n equations, which include n unknowns, a solution is not impossible, that is, a set of values may be found for the unknowns which satisfies all the equations. Unless the equations are linear, which is not likely to be the case, there may not be a unique set of equilibrium populations. The solution may also include values for the x's, population sizes, which are inadmissible, such as negative or imaginary numbers. If an equilibrium is to be achieved in the real world, the equilibrium values of all the various populations must be both real and positive.

The fact that ecological equilibriums do exist, however, at least on a temporary basis, demonstrates that for some combinations of populations an equilibrium solution is achieved. If we have a set of species for which there is no equilibrium solution, then some of the species will die out or new species will come in until there is an ecological equilibrium. Thus, a given pond tends to a certain ecological equilibrium with given numbers of different kinds of fish, algae, vegetation, and even mineral species, such as different salts in the water. If we remove say 20 percent of a given species of fish and do nothing else, if circumstances remain the same, it is likely that this species will expand its population to roughly the previous level in a relatively short time. If however, we remove one of the species altogether, this may disturb the equilibrium so profoundly that other species will also die out until a new equilibrium is achieved.

These principles can be illustrated by simple diagrams in the case of a two-species equilibrium. Here we suppose that all circumstances remain constant and that for each of the two species there will be an equilibrium population for each value of the population of the other species. Three cases may be distinguished.

1. In the case of mutual competition an increase in the population of either species diminishes the population of the other. Suppose we have two species such as lions and tigers living off essentially the same environment. In Figure 2-1*a* we plot the population of lions vertically and the population of tigers horizontally, and we can postulate a "lion curve," *LL'*, showing how many lions there will be in equilibrium for each population of tigers. If there are O*L'* tigers, there will be no lions at all. If there are no tigers, there will be O*L* lions. Similarly, *TT'* is the tiger curve. If there are no lions, there will be O*T* tigers and if there are O*T'* lions, there will be no tigers. In the figure, the curves intersect at point *E*, which is an ecological equilibrium. In this case it is a stable equilibrium at which there will be O*G* tigers and *GE* lions. We can test the stability of the equilibrium position by assuming that in the dynamics of the system with any given combination of lions and tigers the population of ei-

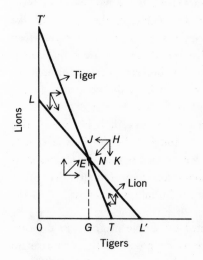

FIGURE 2-1*a*

ther will move toward its own particular equilibrium curve. Thus, suppose we start out from a point such as *H*, in a given period of time the tiger population will move toward the tiger curve, say to *J*, and the lion population will move toward the lion curve to *K*. The resultant change in the system can be seen by filling in the parallelogram, and the total movement will be from *H* to *N*. The arrows in the diagram show that from any position outside *E*, the system will move toward *E*.

Suppose now there is a change in the functions of the system (Figure 2-1*b*), representing, say, a worsening of the competitive position of the lion. Suppose for instance that there is some disease which affects lions but not tigers. The lion curve will shift, say, from *LL'* to *L₁L₁'*. The equilibrium position shifts from *E* to *E₁* with more tigers and fewer lions, as we should expect. If the worsening of the lion's position is severe enough, the lion curve may shift to *L₂L₂'*, at which point the equilibrium population of the lions is zero and the lion would become extinct.

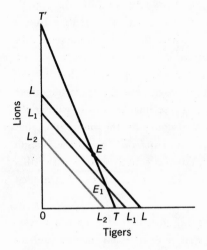

FIGURE 2-1*b*

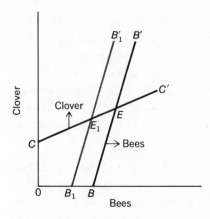

FIGURE 2-2*a*

2. Another possible case is that of mutual cooperation, which is illustrated in Figure 2-2*a*. A good example would be bees and clover.
The more clover there is in a given area, the more bees there will
be. The more the bees, the more the clover will be fertilized and the
more clover there will be. In Figure 2-2*a*, if we measure the population of bees horizontally and clover vertically, we will then have a
bee line *BB'*, suggesting that even if there is no clover, there will be
some bees; the more clover there is, the more bees there will be.
Similarly, there will be a clover line *CC'*, suggesting that even if
there are no bees there will be some clover, but the more bees there
are, the more clover there will be. These lines intersect again at the
point of equilibrium *E*. Here a worsening of the position of one
species, such as a move of the bee line from *BB'* to B_1B_1' will result
in a new equilibrium E_1, at which, however, both species are smaller
in numbers than they were before. The reader can test for himself
that this equilibrium is stable.

A very curious case is suggested in Figure 2-2*b*. Here we have two
species which are so cooperative that both of them may expand indefinitely or at least to very high levels before an equilibrium is

reached. Cases of this sort are virtually unknown in the biosphere, but in the social system some relationships of this kind may exist between man and his artifacts, which explains in large part why the human population has expanded so persistently over the course of human history without showing any sign of reaching an equilibrium. By "artifacts" we mean those populations in man's environment, both internal and external, which he himself creates. These may include knowledge in his internal environment and capital goods in his external environment, starting from primitive stone tools and working up to computers. What the diagrams suggest is that man at some level of his population such as O*A* creates artifacts equal to *AB* which then permit a larger equilibrium human population OC which then creates a still larger quantity of artifacts *CD* and so on. As long as the artifacts curve lies above the man curve the system leads to constantly increasing populations of both without any sign of equilibrium. If there is to be an equilibrium, for instance at *E*, the curves must converge either through man's artifacts becoming less friendly to his increase, which may be happening now with the development of nuclear weapons and pollution, or through the earth becoming so overcrowded that man becomes disorganized and loses his capacity for making further artifacts. At particular

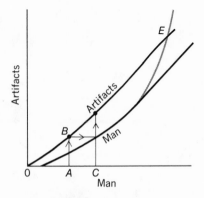

FIGURE 2-2*b*

times and places there seem to have been temporary equilibriums, but so far these have always been broken up by a new uprush of human creativity.

3. A third possible relationship of two populations is that of predation or parasitism in which the first population is cooperative with the second but the second is competitive with the first. This is illustrated in Figure 2-3 with dogs and fleas. Here we measure the number of dogs horizontally and the number of fleas vertically. The flea line FF' suggests that there will be some fleas even if there are no dogs, which is reasonable unless the fleas are extremely highly specialized, and from then on, the more dogs, the more fleas. If there are no fleas, there will be quite a large number of dogs, OD, then the more fleas the fewer dogs. Here again there is equilibrium at point E, the intersection of these two curves. A striking feature of this type of relationship is that it is rather insensitive to changes in the underlying conditions. In the case of Figure 2-1a, which illustrates

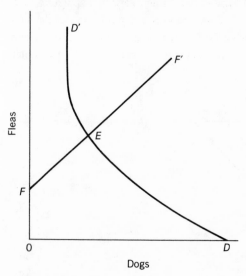

FIGURE 2-3

mutual competition, a relatively small change in the underlying conditions indeed can lead to the extinction of one or the other of the species. Even in Figure 2-2a, a fairly small change in the underlying conditions may lead to large changes in the position of equilibrium, although actual extinction is unlikely. In Figure 2-3, even though an improvement in the dogs' position will increase both the population of dogs and the population of fleas, as the reader may test for himself, and an improvement in the fleas' position will result in more fleas and fewer dogs, these changes are not likely to be very large. This unquestionably accounts for the strong persistence of predation or parasitism in the natural world, and even in social systems.

An equilibrium population is defined as one that neither grows nor declines. In such a population the number of births in a given period must exactly equal the number of deaths, birth being defined as an entry into the population and death a departure from it. It is clear therefore, that the machinery of ecological equilibrium operates through the impact of the set of population counts of different species on the birthrates and the death rates of each one. Thus, we can extend Equations (1) by supposing that for each species I the birthrate B_i is a function of the size of the populations of all the other species and the death rate likewise, as in Equations (2):

$$B_i = F_b\ (x_1, x_2, \ldots, x_n)$$
$$D_i = F_d\ (x_1, x_2, \ldots, x_n) \tag{2}$$

We then have an equilibrium

$$B_i = D_i \tag{3}$$

from which it follows that

$$F_b\ (x_1, x_2, \ldots, x_n) = F_d\ (x_1, x_2, \ldots, x_n) \tag{4}$$

which can easily be rearranged in the form of one of the equations of Equations (1). In biological populations the birthrate of any population is mainly a function of the size and the nutrition and crowd-edness of the population itself, and the death rate is of course a function of predators and also of populations which constitute the food supply.

In Figure 2-4 we show a possible relationship between the birth and death rates of a particular species and the total population of the species itself. Here we measure the total population horizontally along OP and the birth or death rate vertically. If there is no population, obviously there are no births and deaths. Even in a small population the birthrate may be quite high; as the population increases there may be some tendency for births to decline simply due to overcrowding, but this is not necessarily the case. The death rate curve $OD'' D' D$ may easily exhibit a declining phase from D'' to D', as with increasing population the cooperative aspects of the organization of the species itself come into play. We come to a point however at which overcrowding and competition with other species is likely to lead to a rise, and eventually a sharp rise in the death rate, say from

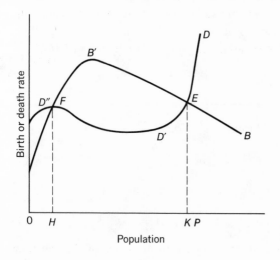

FIGURE 2-4

D' to D. As we have drawn the curves they intersect in two places, at E, which is a stable equilibrium, and at F, which is an unstable equilibrium. A population which is below F, that is OH, will simply die out as the death rate will always be above the birthrate. Populations between OH and OK will increase as the birthrate is above the death rate. Populations beyond OK will diminish as the death rate is above the birthrate. Changes in the environment or in the nature of the species itself may shift these curves. A rise in the birthrate curve represents an improvement in the position of the species in ecological competition. A rise in the death rate curve represents a worsening of the position of the species. If the death rate curve rises to the point where it lies wholly above the birthrate curve, the species will die out, as with any population where the death rate is above the birthrate.

Figure 2-4 may apply to a commodity just as it does to a biological species, though the form of the curves may be different and the machinery of reproduction and even of death very different. In the case of a commodity such as an automobile there is a stock which corresponds to the population in any period of time, there is a production of the commodity which corresponds to births, that is, the number of new units of the species produced, and there is a consumption of the commodity which corresponds to deaths. Automobiles, of course, do not produce other automobiles by mating with each other. Automobiles are produced by a process which involves another set of artifacts, such as mines, mining machinery, transportation equipment, foundries, stamping mills, assembly plants, and so on, and a social organization in the shape of a firm or corporation to administer these artifacts. The automobile factory, however, is the "womb" of the automobile, though whether it actually produces automobiles or not depends on the nature of the social organization which administers it. In a market-type economy it will produce automobiles if their production is believed to be profitable by the owners and administrators of the productive equipment. In a centrally planned economy it will produce automobiles if the decision makers of the economy decide that such production should be part of the plan. Human beings in this case can be regarded as part of the genetic apparatus of the automobile.

The principal difference between biological populations and populations of commodities is that whereas, as we see in Figure 2-4, the major limiting factor in the case of biological populations tends to be the death rate, in the case of commodities it tends to be the birthrate. Thus for automobiles the death rate curve is likely to be something like DD' in Figure 2-5, for the rate at which automobiles are consumed, that is, disappear, is not going to depend very much on the total number though, as we have assumed in the figure, the more automobiles there are the more they run into each other and that hence it is not unreasonable to assume that slightly rising death rate with increase in the population. The birthrate function is likely to be more like BB', with a high birthrate where automobiles are few, perhaps increasing somewhat with an increase in numbers as

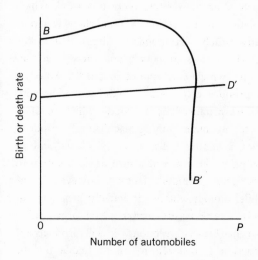

FIGURE 2-5

this stimulates an increase in automobile plants but then declining very sharply once a certain population is reached simply because it is no longer profitable to produce more new cars.

An interesting application of population analysis is the principle of territoriality. Animal species can be divided fairly sharply into two classes—those that limit their population by food shortage and those that limit their population by some form of territoriality. Territoriality means that one animal, or in some cases a pair, or a male with a "harem," and their offspring stake out and defend a certain territory and fight off any members of the same species that try to invade it. The stickleback is an example of this among fish, the robin among birds. There are many examples among animals, and even man shows considerable evidence of this type of behavior, as when he proclaims that his house is his castle. The great evolutionary advantage of territoriality is that it tends to limit the population of a species at a point where it still has an ample food supply. Thus, what might be called the territorial strategy results in a higher "standard of life" than the opposite strategy, which might be called "fecundity," at least in the case of single families. A good example of this would be the difference between the house cat and the alley cat. The population of house cats is limited severely by the number of cat lovers. If a kitten cannot find a niche, that is, a territory, in the home of a cat lover, it will not survive as a house cat. The population of alley cats, by contrast, is only limited by the food supply. If there are too many alley cats, enough of them will starve to bring the population back to equilibrium. It is clear that the house cat has a much higher standard of life than the alley cat. One observes generally indeed that species which are territorial, like the robin, tend to have a rather prosperous appearance, whereas those that are not territorial, like deer, often look hungry.

Another evolutionary strategy is that of being a predatee, that is, a victim of a predator. If enough members of a population get eaten by someone else, the remaining ones may have an adequate food supply for themselves. Deer are an interesting example of this phenomenon. The elimination of predators has often resulted in an expansion of the deer population to the point where nearly all starve.

Territoriality is often observed on a group basis. Here, however, its virtues are much less, for a group may expand within its territory to the point where its population is also limited by the food supply. Group territoriality, therefore, frequently gets the worst of all possible worlds. It involves the species in the fighting which territoriality implies, but it does nothing adequate to limit the population. Human territoriality as reflected in tribes or in national states on the whole falls into this category and from an evolutionary point of view is little to be recommended.

In the analysis of equilibrium populations the interactions between economics and biology have been profound. The principle of population equilibrium was first popularized by Malthus in 1798. Charles Darwin two generations later gave credit to Malthus in the development of some main ideas of the theory of evolution. It is ironic that whereas Malthus thought he was expounding a dynamic system, as for instance in his famous principle that population increases geometrically and the food supply mathematically, his dynamics are quite unsound and have been largely falsified. His vision of an equilibrium of population, on the other hand, is extremely sound and has been abundantly justified. The Malthusian equilibrium can be expounded in the familiar diagram shown in Figure 2-6. Here we measure the size of the population horizontally and a variable which we can call per capita real income vertically. We can postulate a per capita real income curve ABC, under given circumstances of the environment, which shows how large will be the real income for each level of population. As we have drawn it we have supposed that real income rises at first with an increase of population as the capacity to exploit the environment improves. Real income reaches a maximum at B however and declines from then on, simply because with larger populations it becomes harder and harder to extract the requisite in-

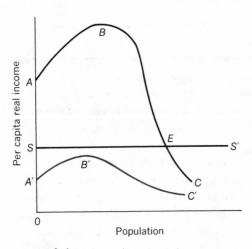

FIGURE 2-6

puts to the population from the environment. We then postulate a subsistence level OS and a subsistence line SS'. The subsistence level is defined as the level of per capita real income at which birth equals death and the population is stationary. In the classical Malthusian model the subsistence level is constant, as represented by line SS', and there is an equilibrium at point E where the subsistence line intersects the per capita real income curve. For any population below the level SE per capita real income is above subsistence and the population by definition will grow. However, if the population is larger than SE, per capita real income will be below subsistence and the population will decline. E therefore is a stable equilibrium. If the conditions of the environment for this particular population are so unfavorable that the per capita real income curve is below the line SS' for all its length, as for instance A'B'C', the population will simply die out as at all levels of population it will be declining.

Malthus and the classical economists generally saw that the subsistence level in the case of the human population is socially rather than biologically determined. Nevertheless, the logic of the Malthusian equilibrium is inescapable and the only possible way to achieve stable levels of human society with a high level of per capita real income is to have a very high subsistence level, that is, an organization that will affect the behavior of people in such a way as to ensure that the population remains stable even at high levels of per capita real income. This is what we mean by population control, which is not the same thing at all as birth control or family planning.

There are a number of possible methods of population control none of which are particularly acceptable at the moment. What might be called the "Irish solution" involves creating a rather deliberate housing shortage and strict family territoriality, so that a couple cannot marry and begin to have children until the old folks die off and leave them the farm. In the Irish case, those who are unable to find a niche in Irish society tend to emigrate. This, however, is clearly not a solution which can be applied to the world as a whole, even in these days of space travel, as it is very clear that the earth is the only decent piece of real estate in a very long way. Another possible but quite unacceptable solution is infanticide, carried out by government order. One could even invent science fiction variants of this such as the death lottery, in which a big holiday would be held every year to kill off exactly enough people to bring the population back to equilibrium. My own suggestion as given in *The Meaning of the Twentieth Century* (Harper & Row, New York, 1964) is sometimes called the "Green Stamp Plan." According to this plan every boy and girl at adolescence is given say 110 green stamps, 100 of which entitle them to have one legal child. We then set up a market in these stamps so that the philoprogenitive and the rich can buy them from the phoboprogenitive (those who do not want to have children) and the poor. The price of these green stamps will automatically achieve a population equilibrium. If the whole society is highly philoprogenitive, the price will be high and that will check the birthrate; if the society is on the whole selfishly concerned with its own pleasure and unwilling to raise children, the price will be low and that will encourage births. As an incidental benefit, the rich will have loads of children and become poor, and the poor will have few children and become rich. If the number of illegal children rises, then the number of stamps received at adolescence will be reduced. The penalty for having an illegal child obviously would have to be some form of sterilization. This modest and humane proposal, so much more humane indeed than that of Swift, who proposed that we eat the surplus babies, has been received with so many cries of anguish and horror, that it illustrates the extraordinary difficulty of applying rational principles to processes involving human generation.

My plan illustrates well the use of the market as a regulator of the great aggregates of society which must be regulated by social means but, at the same time, with a minimum of interference with the behavior of individuals by outside coercion. If you contrast my Green Stamp Plan for population control with what seems to be the only real alternative, the legal limitation of all families to two children, with some exceptions in the case of favored and powerful people, the former, which employs the relatively impersonal pressure of the market, seems much to be preferred to the latter, which calls for the direct coercive intervention of the state, for certainly nobody wants a government inspector coming around and telling him how many children he can have. One sees the same problem in the contrast between the use of the market for the allocation of consumer goods and the imposition of direct rationing which creates administrative problems of an almost insoluble nature and is only tolerable under conditions of extreme social stress, as in war or revolution.

We should take another look at the dynamics of the Malthusian system. It is again one of the ironies of history that Malthus made his gloomy predictions precisely at the moment when the food supply at least of the Western world was going to expand faster than the population for 150 years or more. The dynamics of the system are illustrated in Figure 2-7. Suppose that we start off with a population

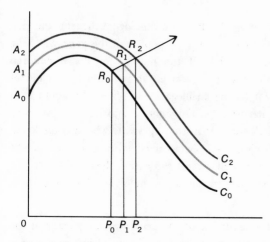

FIGURE 2-7

OP_0 and a per capita real income curve A_0C_0 and a per capita real income P_0R_0. In the next period the population expands to OP_1 but the per capita real income curve rises to A_1C_1 because, shall we say, of technical change or new discoveries so that the per capita real income in this period is P_1R_1. In the next period the population expands to OP_2, but the rise in the per capita real income curve to A_2C_2 results in the rise of per capita income to P_2R_2. This is roughly what has been happening for the last 150 years, at least in the Western world. The real question, of course, is whether the expansion or rise in the per capita real income curve can go on indefinitely. This is what the classical economists were talking about when they referred to "the race between capital and population." They thought that the rise in the per capita real income curve was mainly due to the accumulation of capital. In fact, it has been mainly due to the accumulation of knowledge, although physical capital has naturally played a part.

It is quite conceivable indeed that food may not be the ultimate factor limiting the human population on earth, simply because the increase of knowledge is such a tremendous process, with such an enormous dynamic of its own, that we may easily end up with a world city with each person raising all the food he needs on one-half of his rooftop in food algae tanks and generating all the power he needs on the other half with energy-producing algae. This "Los Angelesation" of the world is indeed a nightmarish vision, but it is by no means off the human agenda. The limiting factor then would be sheer space. The extreme case of course is standing room only, with each human being having only 1 square foot. At the present rate of population growth we will reach this in about seven hundred years and the world Los Angeles is only about three hundred years off. Obviously in what might be called "near-historic time" we must devise some form of population control or the end will be unspeakable disaster. This leads, indeed, to what I have called the "Utterly Dismal Theorem," which states that if the only thing that can check the growth of population is starvation and misery or some other form of low per capita real income, then the long-run consequence of all technical improvement is an enormous expansion of the number of people who live in misery. Fortunately, the dismal Malthusian theorem can be stated in a cheerful form, to the effect that if other things than starvation, misery, low per capita real income, congestion, or whatever undesirable method of population control we would like to cite can limit the population, then the population does not have to grow until all these disastrous things happen. The cheerful theorem, however, involves as an absolute necessity, self-conscious population control on the part of the total society. There is simply no escape from this. This is theorem number one of what might be called ecological economics.

Another very important aspect of ecological economics which is receiving more and more attention is the problem of pollution and exhaustion. Economists frequently tend to dismiss this problem with cheerful platitudes. It is something however, that lies in wait for us in what I have elsewhere called the "spaceship earth," that is, the society which unquestionably lies ahead of us, in which all the easily extractible resources have been extracted, and all the pollutable reservoirs have been polluted, and we will have to revert to a spaceship economy in which everything is recycled. At the moment the economic system is what may be described as a throughput economy. We extract ores and fossil-fuels; we process these into commodities and in doing so we produce negative outputs of pollutants, that is, undesirable products of human activity with a negative value. These we dispose of in pollutable reservoirs, which might almost be called negative mines. This one-way street of the economic system clearly cannot maintain traffic forever. Sometime in human history the mines will be exhausted and the pollutable reservoirs filled up. Resources for the Future estimates that this is just a hundred years away, and after that it is the deluge of junk or the drying up of sources. Here again of course the dynamics of the system may fool us, as in a sense they falsified the predictions of Malthus for 150 years. The growth of knowledge, which is the dominant factor in the present world social system, is still expanding the extractible resources and even the pollutable reservoirs. The sheer payoffs of the economic system guarantee that a large amount of effort will be spent in discovering new resources when old ones become scarce. When wood began to get scarce, we discovered the use of coal; when coal began to get scarce, we discovered the use of oil; when oil showed signs of exhaustion, we discovered nuclear energy, and so on. In the last two hundred years the discovery of new resources has far exceeded the rate of their exhaustion.

It may be indeed that we will find the pollutable reservoirs problem more intractable than the exhaustible resources problem. Los Angeles ran out of air before it ran out of water, and Lake Erie, which used to be a great lake, is now a little cesspool. The habit which man has had ever since he has been around of treating the earth as a great big inexhaustible schmoo may eventually lead to his undoing. There have been plenty of examples on a local scale of societies which have

FIGURE 2-8*a*

collapsed because they ran out of exhaustible resources, either soil or water or ores. It has even been suggested that the decline of the Roman Empire was the result of lead poisoning which resulted from the Romans' own plumbing, which suggests that failure was due to pollution. It would be ironic if our own society were destroyed in the long run by DDT in its irreversible effects. The earth ecologically is a delicate system, even though it is astonishingly resilient within limits. Once the limits are transgressed, however, irreversible processes may easily be set up which will make it impossible for us to return to past Edens.

The problem is illustrated in Figure 2-8*a* and *b*. Figure 2-8*a* shows the throughput economy with the crocodile of human activity eating the exhaustible resources in front and filling up the pollutable reservoirs behind. In the spaceship economy of Figure 2-8*b* the social system has to maintain itself in the middle of a circular flow of materials. We literally will have to eat our own excrement after it has been suitably processed and we have applied energy to the diminution of its entropy.

The concept of what might be called social entropy is of such importance in this connection that one is almost tempted to try to for-

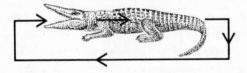

FIGURE 2-8*b*

mulate an entropy theory of value. Unfortunately, we do not have any measure of social entropy as neat as the measure of entropy in thermodynamics, and until we do we must be careful of the analogy. Nevertheless, it is tempting to regard the whole economic process as one by which the world is organized into structures of increasing improbability. The process of production then takes things of higher probability such as soil, ores, and raw materials of all kinds and turns them into much less probable creations such as Volkswagens, pictures from Mars, and cathedrals. At the other end, consumption processes are continually wearing down these improbable structures into more probable structures such as dust, soil, and worms. The total process combines biological organization—in the growth of the person or the animal or the plant—and social organization—in the creation of artifacts and specialized knowledge and education. The labor theory of value derived some of its power from the fact that human activity is an important element in this total process of creating improbability. It is, however, by no means the only process, and it is not the energy involved in manual labor which is significant but the information involved in the human organizing process. Energy is only important in the social process insofar as it can produce an output of negative entropy, that is, an output of more organized and improbable structures. Energy itself is conserved. It is incapable of evolution. It is only as it is used for the segregation of entropy, that is, for the separation of the world into pockets and islands of high organization, at the cost of increasing chaos elsewhere, that it becomes an agent of the evolutionary process. This is as true in economic and social systems as it is in biological systems.

This is a point of great importance which is frequently misunderstood by economists. The throughputs of a system, whether of energy as it moves from forms of high potential to forms of low potential, or of materials in the processes of production and consumption, are essentially *costs* of the system, not rewards or returns. It is true of course that highly developed systems tend to have a high through-

put of energy. The use of energy per capita indeed is highly correlated with per capita real income. Highly developed systems also
tend to have a large volume of production and consumption. The
significant measure of human welfare, however, is not the throughput of energy or materials or even values. It consists of the state and
the environment of the human individual. The difference between a
rich person and a poor person is that the rich person in his bodily
and mental state and in those extensions of his body which lie
around him and over which he has power, such as his house, his automobile, his clothing, and so on is elaborate, complex, and improbable. The poor person occupies a more probable state of ill health,
poor nutrition, poor housing, poor clothing, limited personal freedom, no transportation, and so on. It so happens that there is a high
correlation between the throughput of production and consumption
in a society, as measured for instance by its gross national product,
and the complexity and elaborateness of the state which it maintains
from moment to moment. This high correlation, however, should
not delude us into thinking that these two things are the same thing.
They are in fact very different and they may not even always be
highly correlated.

Thus, economies in consumption, which permit us to maintain the
same state or condition with a smaller throughput of production and
consumption, increase human welfare. The gross national product
might better be called the gross national cost. Actually gross consumption is the cost and the gross product is equal to the consumption plus the excess which may be used for improving the state of
the society. The welfare of the society however should be measured
strictly by its state or condition, that is, by its total capital structure
including its human capital, not by its throughput of production and
consumption, for the gross national product increasingly includes
such unproductive and mainly "maintenance" items as national defense, commuting to work, the replacement of unnecessarily shoddy
commodities, and so on and thus becomes less and less suitable as a

measure of human welfare. International, interregional, or interclass comparisons of gross product, even on a per capita basis, are even more suspect as a measure of relative human welfare. A country under a pleasant climate, with a population adequately nourished and in good health and a culture that promotes cheap, simple, and helpful pleasures may have a much lower per capita GNP than a country with a bad climate, a big defense industry, and a culture which promotes human individual misery. Yet the people of the former society may be much better off than the people of the latter.

An important link between ecological and economic processes, which has been hinted at several times in the course of this chapter, is what might be described as the total metabolic process of the system. Metabolism in a biological organism is parallel to production in an economy. It consists essentially of the transformation of inputs into outputs in accordance with a functional relationship between them. If we know the function and we are given the inputs, we should be able to predict the outputs. Thus, the biological organism has an input of food, gases from the atmosphere, water, minerals, and so on and it has an output of excrement, gases, and ultimately its dead body. Each organism, that is, is a "node" in a great network of inputs and outputs. For a continuing system, as we have seen, the network has ultimately to be circular. The problem of what organisms can survive in a self-sustaining system, however, is related very closely to the nature of the production functions which link the inputs and outputs, that is, the metabolic process.

Here, curiously enough, the economist has perhaps a clearer concept of the process than the biologist. In the economic system the survival of an organization such as the firm depends on its capacity to produce outputs of a total value at least equal to its inputs. There is a proposition, for instance, that in a perfectly competitive market the price of each product in equilibrium will be equal to the average total cost of the marginal firm. The price is the total revenue divided by the output or outputs of the physical commodity, and the average total cost is the total value of all the inputs divided by the output of the physical commodity. This proposition could be stated in another form—that in an equilibrium of the price system the total revenue of each firm must be equal to the total cost, including rent and, of course, the normal remuneration of capital.

Biologists have no measure of biological value as neat as the economist's money. Nevertheless, I suspect that there are parallels in biological ecosystems to the economists' equilibrium price system, in the sense that there is an equilibrium set of inputs and outputs of all kinds. The expansion of a biological species which is below its equilibrium level is a result of something that might be called "biological profit," just as the expansion of a social species, firms producing a given commodity, where the industry is below its equilibrium level, is a result of the fact that the disequilibrium in question is characterized by abnormal profitability of the underexpanded industry. The biological problem of regeneration, whether of populations of species or of limbs or wounds in the case of the individual animal, exhibits so many parallels to what we have called the price-profit mechanism in economics that it is hard to believe that a concept of biological profit would not be useful.

We may conclude the chapter with two important applications of ecological economics. The first is to the problem of the spatial distribution of economic and indeed all human activity. Economic and social activity tend to occupy patterns in space as well as in time which look very much like a general equilibrium. The theory of economic location as developed by writers such as Alfred Weber, Lösch, and Walter Isard has some similarity to the theory of the geographical location of species in biological ecology. The difference between the relatively passive biosphere and the extraordinarily active sociosphere, however, is illustrated by the difference between biological and social location. On the whole the location of biological species is very largely a function of the physical environment. We certainly don't get fish in the desert or cactus in the ocean. On the whole, that is, the biosphere adapts to the physical environment even though it changes that environment somewhat. Thus, the absorption of carbon dioxide from the air in the carboniferous era by the plants which eventually became coal may well have led to the extinction of many of the plants themselves. Similarly, soil everywhere is largely a result of the interaction of the biosphere with the rocks, water, and air which constitute its basic physical environment. The impact of the biosphere on its environment, however, is relatively minor. The impact of the sociosphere on its environment is enormous. For instance, it was shown by Lösch that even if economic activity were uniformly distributed over a uniform plane it would soon structure itself into towns and cities of various sizes with a countryside around them. It is true of course that the exact location of cities and towns is determined by the particular conformation of the physical environment. Mining towns are where the ores are, cities tend to develop at points of transshipment, such as ports, heads of navigable rivers, beginnings of mountain passes, and so on. Nevertheless, the basic pattern of human geographical activity is largely a product of the sociosphere itself.

Thus, like the Roman Empire, countries which are based primarily on a threat system rather than on exchange will have a large capital city with relatively insignificant provincial towns. Commercial countries like the United States, Canada, and Australia, where the principal driving force in society is exchange rather than threat, tend to have small capital cities and large commercial and manufacturing cities. The automobile has transformed the ecological structure of urban life. It is destroying central cities and moving most economic activity into a ring or a "chicken wire" pattern, by contrast with the "classical" city with radial lines of transportation going out into suburbs. The simplest ecological pattern is the ring structure in which the central city is surrounded by concentric rings of economic activity with the furthest rings occupied by those activities which can bear the highest cost of transport or require least in the way of personal interaction. Thus, in the dairy industry liquid milk tends to be produced close to the city, but the milk belt may be surrounded by a cream belt, a butter and cheese belt, and finally a stock-raising belt. As costs of transport diminish and become more flexible however, these patterns break up. We see the same thing happening, as a matter of fact, in the international system; there the old patterns are breaking up under the impact of greatly diminished costs of transport of destruction, which have largely destroyed what I have called the unconditional viability of nations.[1] Examples could easily be multiplied.

Another very important application of the concept of ecological economics is the problem of laissez faire and social planning. The "invisible hand" of Adam Smith is precisely the principle of ecological equilibrium. Adam Smith saw clearly that exchange would operate to produce a division of labor and a constant improvement in productivity even in the absence of any conscious government intervention beyond the minimum requirements of law and order and the fulfillment of contracts. Adam Smith's whole concept of "natural liberty" is an ecological concept. Under a regime of natural liberty, a society will develop specialized occupations and experience economic evolution. The biological world, likewise, operates under a regime of natural liberty and produces specialized species which interact with each other and produce a process of evolution which is unplanned, at least in the sense that the invisible hand does not have to be attached to a head. Similarly, under a regime of laissez faire, economic evolution, that is, development, will proceed by a process of social mutation and selection with the proviso that mutations which seem to increase productivity have a better chance of surviving than those which do not. Hence, there is a bias in the evolutionary process toward development, that is toward increasing productivity.

Nevertheless, the fact that natural liberty is capable of producing development does not mean that "artificial liberty" could not result in development at a faster rate. Nor does it mean that natural liberty

[1] See Boulding, *Conflict and Defense*, Harper & Row, New York, 1963.

will inevitably produce development. An important ecological concept is of relevance here, the concept of ecological succession toward a climax. A biological ecosystem like a pond may be in temporary equilibrium. It will be subject however to certain long-run irreversible phenomena such as a gradual filling in from silt from the rivers that feed it or the absorption of materials from the atmosphere by the plants which surround and inhabit it. If this process goes on long enough the pond will become first a swamp, then perhaps a prairie, and eventually a forest. Some ecosystems are much more stable than others, though no system can be regarded as ultimately stable. In a given physical environment, however, ecological succession often results in a climax, that is, an ecosystem which remains stable for a very long period and will be disturbed only by fundamental evolutionary mutation or major environmental changes. The same thing may happen in society, and under a regime of natural liberty we may get a climactic social system such as the Indian village which is extremely stable, yet in many respects very undesirable.

The point here is that whereas biological systems do not have any option but natural liberty in the absence of man, social systems do have a certain option of social self-consciousness and social intervention, largely through the political mechanism. One can see a parallel here with agriculture. Agriculture consists of distorting the "natural" ecosystems of an environment in favor of man. It means making crops grow instead of thistles, raising domesticated animals instead of wild animals, practicing soil conservation rather than soil erosion, and so on. There is the famous story of the preacher who congratulated a farmer on what he and God had done with his farm. The man replied, "You should have seen it when God had it to himself." Without any disparagement of either the Deity or the laws of nature, it is clear that agriculture, while it means cooperating with the known laws of nature, also means profound intervention in the ecosystem. Social organizations, whether in the form of governments or private organizations, play the role of farmers in regard to the social ecosystem, that is, they distort the social system, hopefully again, in favor of man or at least in favor of the ideals of their decision makers. Thus, the institutions of government try to eradicate social weeds, such as crime and poverty, and encourage the growth of schools, colleges, happy families, and so on.

Just as agriculture implies a knowledge of agronomy, however, social planning implies a knowledge of the true dynamics of society. Our knowledge in this regard is extremely sketchy and it is not surprising, therefore, to find that social plans often produce very different results from what was expected.

The ideological conflict between socialism or the centrally planned economies, on the one hand, and capitalism or the market-dominated economies, on the other, is no longer really a controversy between advocates of planning and advocates of laissez faire. It is rather a controversy over the best methods of deciding, in the first place, which future, out of various alternative futures, the society wishes to move into and, in the second place, which means offer the best prospect of moving the society where it wants to go. On the whole, the socialist societies rely on the ideological dispositions of a small elite communist party to decide the first, whereas the market-type societies are more apt to rely on the broader wishes of the population. In regard to the second, the socialist societies tend to rely on hierarchical and often rather coercive organizations whereas the market-type societies rely more on "social agriculture," that is, using the forces of natural liberty but introducing new pressures, motivations, and rewards largely through the "grants economy," especially through government one-way transfers, so that the result is more to the political satisfaction of the total society. The socialist society is more like a factory and the capitalist society is more like a farm. This perhaps may account for the fact that agriculture is the great failure and the spectacular success of the two societies respectively! The so-called third world of the poor countries of the tropics unfortunately seems to have a remarkable capacity for falling between these two stools. These countries introduce enough intervention in the market, especially through quantitative controls, to destroy the operations of natural liberty and the invisible hand, or at least cut off some of its fingers! At the same time they do not substitute hierarchical centrally planned organizations. The people of these countries, therefore, to use an old crack of the thirties are "more planned against than planning." A major disaster for the human race may very well be brewing in them.

THREE

Economics as a Behavioral Science

The term "behavioral science" was coined quite deliberately in the early 1950s to avoid the identification of the "social" sciences with socialism in the minds of backwoods congressmen. Its slightly dubious origins are reflected in the vagueness of the word "behavioral." In one sense all sciences study the behavior of something, be it electrons, atoms, molecules, viruses, cells, animals, or people. As the term is used in behavioral science it is virtually limited to the study of the behavior of people, with occasional side glances at animals and machines. Behavior itself, however, is a universal concept in science and one of great importance. It is concerned first with the definition of some "behavior unit" which represents a "node" in a network of inputs and outputs. What we mean by behavior then is some kind of relationship between the inputs and outputs of the behavior unit. This concept can also cover the extreme cases where there are inputs without any outputs and outputs without any inputs. There are cases in which inputs are simply absorbed into a behavior unit without producing any immediate outputs at all, and there are cases where the internal activity of a behavior unit produces outputs without any apparent inputs. Usually, however, we observe both inputs and outputs, and if there is any kind of stable functional relationship between them, we have a form of behavior which can be defined. The inputs and outputs are of three broad kinds—matter, energy, and information—and each kind may take a large number of different forms. Most behavior units have inputs and outputs of all three, and all three may be related.

The problem of behavior is enormously complicated by the fact that behavior units have a "state," condition, or structure of their own at any moment of time, which is a result of all previous outputs and inputs and may be the principal source of current outputs. Behavior, that is, is not simply a stimulus-response pattern. Outputs are not necessarily related to immediate inputs. They may be related to inputs many years back. A pure stimulus-response theory of behavior has very grave limitations simply because every response, that is, output, is in a sense a response to all previous stimuli or inputs. A stimulus indeed is a special category of input which has, as it were, a triggering effect on the state of the organization. It is the combination of the trigger plus the state or condition which produces the output or the response. We should not expect to find very simple relationships therefore between immediate stimuli and immediate responses. A pure "black box" behavioral science, which studies only inputs and outputs and makes no attempt to pry off the lid of the behavior unit to see what is inside, suffers from almost fatal limitations.

Even though psychology has been the behavioral science *par excellence*, economics has important contributions to make in this area. The concept of a behavior unit is familiar to economists in the shape of the firm or the household. Economists have been rather slow to recognize that there is a large class of economically relevant behavior units lying somewhere between the firm and the household and having some characteristics of both. These are nonprofit organizations such as schools, universities, hospitals, municipalities, orphanages, old folk's homes, and so on. Governmental organizations, at local, state, national, and international levels, likewise have to be considered as behavior units from an economic point of view, even though the complete study of their behavior is traditionally regarded as in the field of political science.

Because of the old distinction between capital and income, which has a long and quite complicated history in economics, economists are familiar with the distinction between the "stock" aspects of a behavior unit, as reflected in its capital structure, state, or condition, and the "flow" aspects, as reflected in its inputs and outputs. An economist indeed would attempt to define the boundaries of a behavior unit by the existence of something like a balance sheet or position statement and a unified accounting system which provided orderly inputs and outputs of information about it. A position statement consists of an orderly list of the assets, both positive and negative, which pertain to a single economic behavior unit, whether it is a corporation, a family, a hospital, or a governmental body, at a given moment of time. A balance sheet is a position statement in which the various items are valued in terms of a single monetary unit such as the dollar. When figures are available, some algebraic total of positive and negative items can be arrived at. This sum is the net worth of the organization. In accounting convention the positive items are all placed on one side of the balance sheet and the negative items and the net worth on the other side. The balance sheet identity, however, is simply that net worth equals the value of positive assets minus the value of negative assets or liabilities.

An "event" in a behavior unit is always reflected in a change in the position statement, and if the definition of the position statement is full enough, an event may actually be *defined* by a change in the position statement. A large number of different kinds of events may be identified. Some of the principal categories are listed below.

1. *Exchange Events.* An exchange always results in a change in one item of the position statement, balanced by an equal opposite

change in another item, so that the net worth remains unchanged. Thus, we may have a purchase of raw materials for $1,000 cash. This is reflected in the balance sheet by a decline of $1,000 in a cash item and an increase of $1,000 in a raw materials item. The purchase of $1,000 worth of labor will result in a decline of $1,000 in a cash item, and an increase of $1,000 in the inventory of materials in process. If the behavior unit borrows $1,000, this is reflected in an increase of $1,000 in a cash item and an increase of $1,000 in some item of liabilities, such as notes payable. As liabilities are negative assets, this again leaves the net worth unchanged.

2. *Internal Transformations.* Exchange involves an output to and an input from the outside environment. Thus when the firm purchases raw materials, it increases its stock of raw materials by means of an input from outside and it diminishes its stock of cash by means of an output of cash to the outside. There may also be internal exchanges which result mainly from transformations in production. Thus when a miller grinds wheat into flour, he diminishes his stock of wheat and increases his stock of flour. The effect on the balance sheet is very much the same as if he had simply exchanged wheat for flour. In the case of exchange, however, there would be inputs to and outputs from the outside world, whereas in the case of internal transformations there are not. When items in the balance sheet are valued "at cost," this means that there have been diminutions in other positive items of the balance sheet, or increases in negative items, equal to the value which is recorded. Thus, suppose the miller records $1,000 worth of flour at cost in his books. This means that somewhere along the line, let us say, $500 worth of wheat has disappeared, $400 worth of cash has gone to purchase labor and has disappeared, and $100 worth of equipment has been depreciated.

3. *Revaluations.* Another important kind of event in the economic behavior unit is the revaluation of assets or liabilities. When this happens there is a change in the net worth. Thus, suppose a firm has an uninsured fire loss of $1,000. Some item on the asset side, such

as buildings or inventories, will be diminished by $1,000, and the net worth will likewise be diminished by $1,000. In the usual accounting convention sales usually involve a combination of exchange and revaluation. Before it is sold, an inventory of finished product is valued at cost since it has resulted from a succession of exchanges and transformations which may not change the firm's net worth. At the moment of sale it is revalued to the amount that it fetches and then exchanged for cash or perhaps accounts receivable. Thus, suppose we have an amount of finished product valued at cost at $1,000 and this is sold for $1,500. What happens to the balance sheet is that $1,000 worth of finished product is subtracted, $1,500 cash is added, and $500 is added to the net worth. Essentially, we can break this down into two events—a revaluation of the finished product to $1,500, which involves an increase in the net worth of $500, and then an exchange of $1,500 worth of finished product for $1,500 cash.

4. *Distributions.* Another category of events in the economic behavior unit consists of distributions, that is, one-way transfers. Usually these consist of transfers of cash to owners in which case the cash item diminishes and the net worth diminishes by an equal amount. Distributions may also be made to and by foundations or for various charitable purposes. There may also be positive distributions in the shape of gifts received. These are uncommon in the case of profit-making organizations, but they are quite common in the case of households and nonprofit organizations. In any case the distribution is always characterized by a one-way transfer of assets and a corresponding change in net worth.

Almost all events which affect the balance sheet will fall into one or another of these four categories, either singly or in combination. This however does not exhaust the total position statement or all the inputs and outputs of the economic unit. The total position statement has to include not only the items of the balance sheet in an accounting sense, but also non-accounting items, such as the organizational structure, the relevant character of the various role occupants in the organizational structure, the internal communication system, and the "knowledge structure" or images of the world in the minds of the decision makers. A very important aspect of the knowledge structure is the perception on the part of the decision makers of the environment and the opportunities provided by the environment. Part of this perception is an image of the exchange opportunities which the environment provides. This might almost be described as the production function of the environment, since it answers the question, if the economic unit puts out certain outputs into the environment, what inputs will it be able to extract from it? The unit's exchange opportunities with the environment may be of several kinds.

We can distinguish first between perfect and imperfect markets in the exchange environment. Where the environment presents a perfect market, this means that an exchange opportunity presents itself at a given price or terms of trade which is independent of the volume of exchange. This is illustrated in Figure 3-1 where we suppose

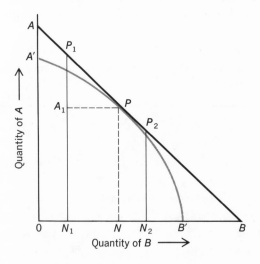

FIGURE 3-1

two assets, A and B, and measure the quantity of B possessed horizontally and that of A possessed vertically. The position statement is represented by point P at which the economic unit has ON of B and NP of A. An exchange opportunity with a perfect market is then represented by the line APB, the slope of which is equal to the ratio of exchange. Thus the unit may go from P to P_1 exchanging B for A, giving up PA_1 of B and receiving A_1P_1 of A, and ending up with stocks of ON_1 of B and N_1P_1 of A. The ratio of exchange is then

$$\frac{A_1P_1}{A_1P}$$

In a perfect market the exchange opportunity line is straight, with a constant slope or rate of exchange. In an imperfect market, the exchange opportunity line would look like the dotted line $A'PB'$. As we move in any direction from P, the terms of trade, that is, how much we get in return for one unit that we give up, worsen. As we exchange B for A, moving toward A', we get less and less A for units of B given up; as we move from P toward B', exchanging A for B we have to give up more of A for each unit of B received. Imperfection may also take the form of discontinuities in the exchange opportunity. Thus, if we had a quota system which only permitted the unit ON_2 amount of B, the exchange opportunity line would become AP_2N_2 and at P_2 the price of B would become virtually infinite.

Exchange opportunities can also be classified as immediate and deferred exchanges. In an immediate exchange, the exchanger gives something into the exchange environment and gets something in return without any perceptible time interval between these two events. Ordinary purchase and sale of commodities is of this type. In deferred exchange there is a significant time interval between the two transfers which constitute the exchange. The exchanger may either give something up now in the expectation of receiving something later or receive something now in the expectation of giving up something later. It is on deferred exchange that the whole financial system is built. A financial instrument such as a share of stock, a bond, or a promissory note creates, on the part of the owner, an expectation of receiving something in the future. In a loan transaction, for instance, the lender usually pays money to the borrower at the present moment in return for a promise on the part of the borrower to pay a larger sum at some date in the future. A deferred exchange can usually be regarded as a combination of two transactions: an immediate exchange, usually of money for a financial instrument or promise, such as a note or a bond, and a deferred exchange, which is consummated when the promise implied in the financial instrument is fulfilled. Promises, in this context, are of two broad kinds—specific promises such as are involved in promissory notes or bonds and conditional promises such as are implied in a share of stock, which is a right to receive a proportion of the distributed profits of a corporation. Deferred exchange, like immediate exchange, may involve both perfect or imperfect markets.

Just as an economic unit has an image of its external environment, so it will have an image of its internal environment which consists essentially of its production functions, that is, the possible set of internal transformations it can perform, or how much output or product it can obtain by the sacrifice of how much of the inputs that go into making it. The miller knows, for instance, usually out of long experience, how many bushels of wheat turn into how many bushels of flour and what additional costs have to be incurred in the process.

The events which constitute the record of the history of an organization may be divided into passive events, which require no decisions and are not under the control of the organism, like depreciation in the case of the firm or aging in the case of a person, and active events, which are under the organism's control.

In the economist's view, an active event consists of an act of choice or a decision on the part of some decision maker among alternative future sequences of events. It is important to recognize that what all decision makers are deciding about are alternative images of the future in their own minds. A decision then results in action which is believed to be related to these images of the future. A decision therefore involves two different aspects of the image of the future in the mind of the decision maker—the image of the alternatives themselves on the one hand and the evaluation of those alternatives on the other. To the economist behavior is "maximizing behavior." He visualizes a decision maker as contemplating a set of alternative images of the future, ordering these first, second, third, etc., or best, second-best, third-best, and then selecting the one which is at the top of his list and acting accordingly. In its most general sense the theory of maximizing behavior is a tautology; it simply says that people do what they think is best at the time, which nobody can deny. If the theory is to have any content and be of any use to anyone, either in the actual process of decision making itself or in the creation of more realistic and complex images of the future, such as images which involve the consequences of other people's decisions, it must include a "learning process."

In its simplest form learning is the process by which inputs of information in the past lead to images of the future in the present. It has been one of the main weaknesses of economic decision theory that it has almost entirely neglected the problem of information, perhaps because it was first formulated on the assumption of perfect markets in the environment, in which case the information problem is not difficult. When an economic decision maker is faced with a perfect market, all that he needs to know is the price or exchange ratio at which exchange can take place in the environment. This information is fairly easy to acquire, as when we go to the store and see the price tags on the goods displayed. Where there are imperfect markets, as there frequently are, the information problem becomes much more difficult; if the environment is changing it becomes still more difficult, for what we found out about the environment yesterday may not apply to it tomorrow. Under these circumstances, an adequate theory of decision making has to include some sort of relationship between the experience of past decisions and the process by which images of the future are built up. It has to include, that is, a feedback from disappointments. Economists, however, do not generally think in these terms, which is perhaps the major reason for a certain sense of dissatisfaction, which is now widespread, with formal economic decision theory.

Just as we have ventured on the classification of possible events, so we may venture on the classification of decisions. The attempt to find a single rule of decision which will cover all categories may be futile, for each category of decisions presents its own special problems. However, we can start off with the categories of events. Where decisions relate to exchange, they are concerned with how far and in what direction the economic unit should proceed along an exchange opportunity line. The same principle goes for internal transfers, which are from the point of view of the behavior unit itself very similar to exchange. A movement along an opportunity line such as AB in Figure 3-1 is made in the hope or expectation of subsequent profitable revaluations. The purest form of economic decision here is in pure speculation in which the economic unit tries to take advantage of changes in the market opportunity lines, that is, changes in market prices. This is illustrated in Figure 3-2 where the axes are the same as in Figure 3-1. We suppose that an economic unit starts at P_0 and exchanges A for B down to P_1; then the price of B rises and it trades B for A up to P_2; then the price of A rises and it trades A for B to P_3. By a succession of processes of this kind it is really increasing its stocks and its net worth. This indeed is the essence of the profit-making process, and the lines in Figure 3-2 could equally well represent alternations of production and sale. In the environment of the perfect market the only thing which limits the amount exchanged for the individual is uncertainty. If for instance in Figure 3-2 the decision maker were

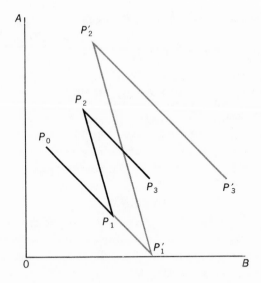

FIGURE 3-2

certain of the changes in the opportunity lines, he would do better to increase the size of the "swings" in his asset composition from P_0 to P'_1 to P'_2 to P'_3. If he could borrow indefinitely in perfect markets he could increase the swings beyond the limits of lines OA and OB. With perfect markets where there is no uncertainty, indeed, the rate of profit could theoretically be infinite, which is absurd. Obviously, then, actual behavior is limited by uncertainty. For instance, as the speculator moves from P_0 down toward P_1 or P'_1 in the expectation of a rise in the price of the asset which he is accumulating, in this case B, he is aware that the loss he stands to suffer if his expectation is wrong is increasing. At the point where the fear of potential loss becomes too great he will stop. This illustrates a very important principle, that under circumstances of uncertainty the fear of loss is a more powerful determinant of behavior than the hope of gain. This principle emerges again in the "minimax" principle in game theory. Thus, a rule of behavior emerges here; move your assets into the type of property you think is going to rise most rapidly in value, up to the point at which you can no longer bear the contemplation of the loss you will sustain if you are wrong. This is a pretty good rule for all decision making, but it is particularly valuable in decisions involving exchange.

Strictly speaking, revaluations stem from the external environment, and while the anticipation of revaluations is an important element in the decision-making process, revaluations themselves result from the decisions of others. Therefore, from the point of view of the individual decision maker they are random processes and not part of the decision-making process itself. Decisions in regard to distributions, however, are up to a point under the control of the decision makers of the economic unit. There is, as a matter of fact, no very good theory to explain the magnitude of distributions. It is not too difficult to formulate a mathematical utility theory which is not much more than an elegant way of saying that organizations distribute as much as they think fit or stop distributing further at the point where they feel that the advantages of additional distributions are not worth the disadvantages, whatever they may be. In the case of the firm, distributions, for instance, to stockholders, diminish the net worth of the firm and the total capital which the managers of the firm have under their control. If profits are not distributed, the value of the stock should rise by approximately the amount of the undistributed profits. Stockholders should be able to make their own distributions by selling off pieces of stock. Although equality between the increase in a company's net worth and the increase in the market price of its stock is by no means realized in practice, it is realized well enough, so that stockholders are usually fairly tolerant of undistributed profits, and there is a strong tendency for successful corporations to grow by not distributing profits, that is, by retaining much of the increase in net worth in the business.

In the case of institutions like the household or even the nonprofit organization or the foundation, distributions represent "grants" and may take the form of charitable donations or the support of relatives. The grants economy, as we noted earlier, is an increasing part of the total economic system and has been very little studied. It is related closely to the identification of mutual interests. It depends, that is, on the sense of community and the nature of personal identity. Economists here are in somewhat unfamiliar territory in spite of the fact that the grants economy now occupies 10 to 15 percent of the American economic system.

An aspect of decision making which has only recently received much attention from economists may be described as the problem of "search." This is the problem of how far it pays to devote costly resources to the improvement of information inputs and thus the improvement of images of the world, especially images of the future. The problem may be put in another way by asking, "How far does it pay to reduce uncertainty, and at what point do we stop trying to reduce it and simply put up with it or adapt our behavior to it?" This, unfortunately, is a question of great importance without any easy answers and one that is very fundamental in the human learning process. If at first you don't succeed, do you try, try again, as the proverb suggests? Or do you say, "To hell with it" and try something else? When you develop that sense of increasing uneasiness which arises from the fear that you are on the wrong road, do you persevere in the hope of getting through to more familiar territory or do you go back to where you got lost? If you are looking for something and cannot find it, at what point do you decide that the thing is not there to be found and abandon the search? How do we decide indeed that something is there to be found? Many of the answers to these questions depend on clues and cues which are often subtle and hard to analyze. Some empirical studies have suggested (see especially Cyert and March, *The Behavioral Theory of the Firm*) that dramatic or salient events often distort the attention span of decision makers and lead to a poor sampling of the field of choice itself.

This suggests another question for decision theory; the problem of information overload. A decision maker has only a certain span of attention and cannot hold more that a certain number of alternatives in mind. If the actual number of alternatives is overly large, it has to be reduced by some sampling process. The structure of an organization is designed in large part to reduce the number of alternatives which are placed before decision makers as we go up the hierarchy. Where there are no simple decision rules, organizations often create arbitrary rules. A possible theory of decision making, one which is a serious competitor to the theory of maximizing behavior, is that faced with overload a decision maker eliminates alternatives arbitrarily until there is only one left and that becomes the decision. Decision making in foundations often seems to follow this pattern. Even in the firm, however, there is a certain amount of folk wisdom to the effect that the main function of top executives is to decide what the firm does not do and thereby to limit the field of choice.

With all these reservations and qualifications one can still put up a good defense for the proposition that the theory of maximizing behavior makes an important contribution to the understanding of human behavior over a wide area. In the last twenty-five years a number of techniques in what might be called "management information systems" have been developed which have applications in many different kinds of organizations and which use what are essentially the principles of maximization. They are directed, that is, toward developing an information system which will assist the decision maker in finding the "best" out of various possible alternatives by identifying some quantity which can serve as a measure of desirability and then finding out what combinations of other variables under his control will lead to the most desirable situation. Linear programming and its various extensions is one such technique. (See page 107.) This is essentially a method for finding those quantities of inputs which will produce a given beneficial output at the least cost or the greatest beneficial output for a given cost. Techniques of cost-benefit analysis in the case of investment projects and what is called "program budgeting" in the case of departmental programs in government or business are likewise attempts to develop information systems which will help the decision maker make the "best" decisions. The development of the computer has made a great many things possible in information processing which were not possible before. Thus, the principles of maximizing behavior suddenly seem more realistic both as a guide and a normative principle in assisting people in making actual decisions and as a description of what people actually do.

The weakness of the traditional marginal analysis which postulated that businessmen would maximize their profits was that the data on which decisions were supposed to be made often did not exist. If a firm does not know what effect a given decision will have on its profits, obviously it cannot maximize profits. We can never climb the top of a mountain if we do not know whether we are going up or down.

Nevertheless, information systems are improving, and it is one of the virtues of the theory of maximizing behavior that it does insist on the importance of what has come to be called incrementalism. Lindblom and Dahl indeed have elevated what they call disjointed incrementalism into a prime political virtue.[1] In effect this means saying, "Let's not bother about being at the top, let's just find which way is up," and this is often very good advice. When we are climbing in a dense fog, as most decision makers are most of the time, we take a tentative step and if our foot goes down we do not make it and if it goes up we do. One of the problems of decision making in conflict systems, especially one such as the international system, is that the decision maker quite literally does not know which way is up and hence often ends up by going down, if the reader will forgive me for stretching the English language to the point of insanity.

[1] Robert Dahl and Charles E. Lindblom, *Politics, Economics and Welfare*, Harper, New York, 1953.

Incrementalism, however, whether disjointed or not, is not enough for it too often leads to a perverse dynamic process in which everybody becomes worse off. The arms race in the international system is a good example of this sort of process, so is the price war in oligopolistic market competition. Quarrels and factional disputes within an organization are other examples. If we are to avoid perverse dynamic processes, we must look beyond incrementalism to some kind of long-range vision that can penetrate the fog and permit us to view more distant summits.

Game theory, which is in a sense an offshoot of the economic theory of maximizing behavior, throws some light on these problems though it has a tantalizing way of breaking down just as one expects its greatest insight. The most general concept of the "game" is a situation in which there are at least two parties and the outcomes or payoffs of the decisions of each party depend on the decisions of the other. This can be represented in a matrix as in Figure 3-3. Here we have two parties that we can call "Column" and "Row." C_1, C_2, . . . , C_n represent decisions or "strategies" of a Column, and R_1, R_2, . . . , R_n are decisions or strategies of a Row. A strategy is just a decision about a set of decisions, and for the purposes of this analysis it can be regarded as a single decision. Then c_{11} represents the payoff to Column when Column is at strategy C_1 and Row

Column \ Row	R_1	R_2
C_1	c_{11} r_{11}	c_{21} r_{12}
C_2	c_{12} r_{21}	c_{22} r_{22}

FIGURE 3-3

is at strategy R_1. r_{11} is the corresponding payoff to Row. The whole matrix of such payoffs is the total field of information on which decisions have been made. Each party, however, has to make his decisions in the light of what he thinks the other party's decisions will be. Therefore neither party can simply take the other's decisions for granted and make the decision which maximizes his own payoff, for the effect of his decision may be nullified by the decision of the other party. Here a good deal may depend in practice on whether decisions are sequential and irrevocable. It is one of the weaknesses of game theory, as it is of the theory of maximizing behavior, that it tends to assume the knowledge problem, which is often the really critical problem of the sequence of decisions. The question is, how do people know what the payoffs are? The answer to this is frequently by trial and error, that is by making decisions and having some kind of feedback from them. This sort of process, however, is completely neglected in ordinary game theory.

Nevertheless, game theory does illuminate many problems of decision making under conditions of uncertainty and conflict. It has established itself as an independent field of study so that there is some doubt as to whether we should include it in economics, in spite of the fact that the classic work in the field by Von Neumann and Morgenstern is entitled *The Theory of Games and Economic Behavior*. We can certainly, however, consider game theory as an extension of the economic theory of decision making as it tries to formulate certain rational principles of decision making under conditions of uncertainty, that is, under conditions where the outcome of a decision depends on the decisions of two or more people. There are roughly three fields of game theory—the first a study of two-person zero-sum games, the zero-sum game as the name implies being one in which in any box of the matrix the sum of the payoffs, say, c_{11} and r_{11} in Figure 3-3, is zero, that is, whatever one party gains, the other party loses. If one party has a positive payoff of x, the other has a negative payoff of x. This is really the only type of game the theory of which has been worked out exhaustively. Unfortunately, it is not a very interesting type of situation in practice, because nobody in their senses would play a zero-sum game. A constant-sum game in which the sum of the payoffs of the two parties is constant, though not necessarily zero, exhibits many of the properties of the zero-sum game, but unfortunately it is also likely to be rare in the real world. By far the commonest type of situation is the variable-sum game in which there are no restrictions on the sum of the payoffs of the two parties for any two strategies or decisions. A third type of game is the so-called n-person game, with more than two players or participants. When we go to even as small a group as three persons, the situation becomes very different from what it was with two persons, simply because of the possibility of coalitions. The n-person game is very largely concerned with the theory of coalitions, that is, with the question, whom does it pay to gang up with whom, against whom. Unfortunately, the results of the theory of the n-person game seem to be singularly devoid of content and are very inconclusive.

The variable-sum two-person game has turned out to be a useful model in the empirical study of certain aspects of human behavior, due especially to the pioneering work of Dr. Anatol Rapoport. A particularly interesting two-person variable-sum game goes under the name of "The Prisoners' Dilemma" because it was originally illustrated by a little story about two prisoners, each of whom had the choice of being silent or "squealing" on the other. If both are silent, then neither will be convicted and both will be better off; if one is silent, however, it pays the other one to squeal; when one squeals it pays the remaining one to squeal. The choices can be generalized into two decisions which we can call "good" and "bad." The sequence of events is illustrated in Figure 3-4 in which we suppose that each party can make two decisions, good or bad. If both are good, each gets payoffs of 10. However, if Column remains good, it pays Row to be bad, as he will then get 20. Similarly, if Row stays good, it will pay Column to be bad. If Row is bad, however, it pays Col-

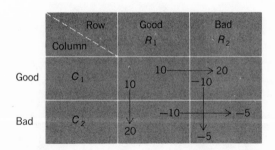

FIGURE 3-4

umn to be bad also, for he will then improve his payoff from -10 to -5. Similarly, if Column is bad, it will pay Row to be bad. The arrows in the figure show the direction of the more favorable decision. Under these circumstances it is clear that everybody will end up in the bad-bad box at the bottom right-hand corner, in spite of the fact that both parties would be better off if they were both good in the top left-hand corner. This is a very simplified model of what I have called the "perverse dynamic" which leads to everybody becoming worse off. Rapoport's experimental work suggests that in a large number of trials people do learn to be cooperative and to stay in the good-good box in spite of the temporary attractions of being bad, that is, the perverse dynamic depends on a kind of shortsightedness and a possible recipe for it is the development of longsightedness through some kind of learning process. The game matrix has thus amply proved its value as a tool for setting up certain problems in human behavior and for creating hypotheses which are especially useful in the study of responsive behavior.

Economists have always been interested in the problem of how people and institutions would respond to perceived changes in their environment if they were following principles of economic behavior. A good deal of economic analysis uses response functions such as those represented by demand and supply curves. A demand curve or function asserts that there is a relationship between the price of a commodity and the amount people will purchase, either individually or in the aggregate. From the point of view of behavior a change in price has to be regarded as a change in the information input of the behavior unit which leads the behavior unit to change its expectations about the environment. Thus if there is a perfect market, a change in price means that the behavior unit perceives a change in its environment equivalent to a shift in the slope of its exchange opportunity line. In the theory of demand it is shown how a demand function can be derived from the underlying preference functions which describe the preferences of the demander, and we can show on very reasonable assumptions that the demand curve will usually have a negative slope, that is, less will be bought at high prices than at low, though there may be exceptions to this.

The supply curve or function is likewise a behavioral response to a perceived change in the exchange opportunity, this time the behavior being the quantity offered for sale. Ordinarily it can be shown that more will be offered for sale at high prices than at low, that is, the supply curve will have a positive slope. There may be important exceptions to this rule also. The empirical study of these response functions presents many difficulties. Nevertheless, a good deal of work has been done along these lines by econometricians. Experimental work is not easy in this area and we generally have to deduce the nature of responses either by studying different responses at different times under different conditions or by making cross-sectional studies of the different responses of different people at different places.

A very important parameter of the response function is its elasticity, relative or absolute,[2] which is a measure of the responsiveness of the responder. If a given change in price, for instance, produces a

[2] Relative elasticity is the percentage change in the responding variable which results from a 1 percent change in the stimulating variable. Absolute elasticity is the absolute change in the former which results from a unit absolute change in the latter.

large change in either the quantity demanded or the quantity supplied, we say the function is elastic, that is, responsive. Response is an important aspect of human behavior in all fields and is always important in determining the general dynamics of the social system. Systems which are responsive, that is, systems in which a given perceived change in the environment produces a large change in behavior, are apt to be much more dynamically unstable than systems which are unresponsive. Some of the concepts of economics here are capable of generalization to many other fields, for instance, response to perceptions of hostility or conflict, response to affection or benevolence, response to persuasion, and so on. We can claim therefore that the economic concept of elasticity is one of a general class of important behavioral concepts which have badly been neglected by other social sciences.

A distinguished social psychologist once chided me by saying, "You think prices are determined by demand and supply, but I know they are determined by people." It is quite true that prices, like every other aspect of economic and social life, are the result of decisions by people, and economists would do well never to forget this. Nevertheless, in analyzing problems such as the determinants of the price system, the behavior of people must be expressed in a simplified form and especially in a form which is capable of aggregation. In these terms the economist can make a strong defense of his demand and supply curves as singling out the significant aspects of the behavior of people from the point of view of that segment of the system in which he is interested.

A final point as regards behavioral economics is that something can be learned from the study of the behavior, especially over time and space, of abstract economic variables—prices, the price level, employment and unemployment rates, exports and imports, and so on —as such. On the whole it is the behavior of economic variables that economists study, not the behavior of people at all. Thus if stock prices rise, this phenomenon certainly originates in the behavior of the people who buy and sell stocks and represents a change in their behavior or at least a change in their state of mind. The empirical economist, however, simply looks at time series of prices and asks how they behave. Similar questions can be asked of regions and nations. I recall that when I was working as an economist for the League of Nations studying European agricultural statistics, I was severely taken to task by my superior for writing that "France behaved differently from Germany," referring to its behavior with regard to things like yield per acre of crops. My superior drew himself up with great dignity and said, "France does not behave, it is a great nation." Nevertheless, I would defend this use of the word, for people or even demigods like nations are not the only things that behave, and it is quite legitimate to talk about and to study the behavior of abstract variables of all kinds. Of course, when studying the behavior of abstract variables, we must never forget that they *are* abstract and that there is a profound difference between something like celestial mechanics and economics or the other social sciences. In the case of celestial mechanics we can neglect the problem of whether the planets are moved by angels without causing any trouble at all for it is only the behavior of abstract time series of the positions of the planets that we are concerned with. In the case of economic and social systems, however, the "planets," that is, the commodities, prices, and other statistical and abstract numbers with which we deal, are in fact moved by people who are not so well-behaved as angels, and we forget this fact at our peril.

Somebody at the Center for Advanced Study of Behavioral Sciences suggested, in a jesting mood, that economics is the study of the no-person group, being the study of the movements of commodities and prices in the absence of people. It is true of all the social sciences, however, that the further they get away from people the more abstract they become and the more scientific they look. Psychology is not much closer to people than economics, as the student in beginning psychology rapidly discovers, often to his discomfiture. Sociology, likewise, concentrates very heavily on abstract measurement. A student who wants to study people indeed had probably better get out of the social sciences altogether and go into literature. In these days I am not even sure whether you will find people there! What all this involves is not a case against abstraction, which is essential, but a warning against mistaking abstraction for reality. We would be foolish to try to go for a walk across a map, but a map may be very helpful if we are going for a real walk.

FOUR

Economics as a Political Science

It is no accident that the old name for economics was political economy. All the classical economists called it by that name. The name economics indeed did not come into general use until the second half of the nineteenth century, as economics became more sharply differentiated from political science and sought to establish its own autonomy as a discipline. Nevertheless, the interrelation between political science and economics continues to be of great importance. Indeed, at the present time there is some question as to whether the two sciences are not showing signs of amalgamating again, perhaps into economic politics rather than into political economy.

As we look around at the flora and fauna of the social system we tend to make a rough classification of economic and political organizations. The Congress of the United States or a state legislature would seem to be clearly political, whereas a corporation or a bank would seem to be mainly economic. Nevertheless, there is a large population of hybrids, such as the Federal Reserve System, the Tennessee Valley Authority, the Social Security System, and the Securities and Exchange Commission. Furthermore, it is clear that even the most political organization has very important economic aspects. A national state could not exist without a large matrix of exchange relationships. An armed force relies on the market for most of its supplies, even if under conscription it relies on the threat system for its personnel. The whole study of public finance, that is, the economic relationships of political organizations, is generally regarded as being in the province of economics. Furthermore, all organizations have important political aspects. The corporation is constantly exercised by constitutional and legal problems, both internal and external, and the problem of how people rise into powerful positions and how decisions are made collectively is essentially political, rather than economic, in nature. If we look at something like the labor movement, which ordinarily is regarded as primarily part of the economic system, we find that it also has extremely important political overtones, not only from the point of view of political power, especially in democratic societies, but also from the point of view of the political structure of trade unions themselves, which exhibit almost every conceivable variety of political form from two-party, representative democracy to absolute dictatorship and tyranny. Every organization, indeed even the family, has a political aspect in its internal role-filling and collective decision-making activities.

If we were to ask ourselves what the prime characteristics of the political aspects of the sociosphere are, the answer might run along at least three different lines. In the first place, political organizations, as opposed to economic organizations, rely for their survival more on a threat system—especially what might be a legitimated threat system—than on an exchange system. In their economic aspects we think of political organizations as organizations that have tax power. The actual status of a tax payment in the social system is a surprisingly complicated one, but it is certainly very different from that of an exchange. Whether we wish to regard taxes as part of "the grants economy" may be a matter of taste in the use of words, but certainly taxes belong to what might be called the "transfer economy." Tax payments differ from exchanges in that they represent one-way transfers of exchangeables from a taxpayer to a tax receiver, and though it can be argued that something passes in return, what passes in return is usually not regarded as an asset by the taxpayer, even though it may be a condition which affects the security or the valuation of his other assets, such as the maintenance of law and order. A tax payment as a one-way transfer, therefore, represents a transfer of assets from the taxpayer to the tax receiver in that the net worth of the taxpayer diminishes and that of the tax receiver increases when a tax is paid. Indeed because of the cost of collecting taxes the taxpayer's loss in net worth is usually greater than the tax receiver's gain in net worth. It has been a cardinal principle of economics since the days of Adam Smith that this difference should be as small as possible. This is indeed the main principle behind the famous "Canons of Taxation," which were enunciated by Adam Smith and have constituted part of the corpus of economics ever since his time.

A question of great interest, but considerable difficulty, is the extent to which taxes are to be regarded as quasi-voluntary, in the sense that in a democratic society, at any rate, we vote our own taxes, or at least vote for the representatives who impose them. There is a principle here that might be called the principle of self-coercion. Whenever we have a situation such that if everybody contributes something, everybody benefits, but if most people contribute, the people who do not contribute continue to benefit, then the use of socially organized threats to insure universal compliance is likely to be regarded as highly legitimate. The issue here might be called, borrowing a term from trade unionism, the "free-loading" problem. If the man who does not join the union and pay dues receives the benefits of union activity, this creates a quite understandable urge on the part of the good unionists to force him to conform through some form of union security, such as the union shop. Even something that is supposed to be a purely voluntary effort, such as a United Fund campaign, often produces strong pressures for universal conformity. Up to a point, therefore, is it not unreasonable to regard at least some taxes as quasi-voluntary, with a compulsory element introduced to ensure universal conformity and get rid of free loading.

A second aspect of the social system which could well be regarded as political is that which involves the allocation of resources among different occupations and employments and the distribution of the product among different claimants. There is a fairly strong tendency among economists to regard the allocation problem as economic and the distribution problem as political. We recall Lasswell's famous definition of politics: "who gets what, when and where." The corresponding definition of economics might be "who does what, when, and where." Thus we find in many textbooks of economics the definition of economics as the study of the allocation of scarce resources, and economists have often taken a line of strict self-abnegation in regard to the distribution of property and income. The allocation of allocation to economics and distribution to politics seems like a neat economic solution to a problem of disciplinary territoriality. Unfortunately, when it is examined carefully the neatness largely disappears.

The real trouble is that in practice it is very hard to separate allocation and distribution. We can see this by examining the effects of possible changes in the relative structure of prices. Suppose, for instance, that the price of wheat rises relative to other things, whether through the operation of market forces or through government intervention and subsidy. This will alter not only the allocation of resources, but also the distribution of income and even property. A relative rise in the price of wheat will make wheat production more attractive, and we may expect that resources will be diverted into it which might otherwise have gone into alternatives, such as the production of other cereals or the raising of cattle. At the same time the rise in the price of wheat will increase the relative real incomes of wheat producers and diminish the real incomes of wheat consumers.

This in turn will increase demand for things that wheat producers have a big demand for, relative to wheat consumers, and diminish the demand for things that wheat consumers have a big demand for, relative to wheat producers. By the time we have followed the repercussions of these effects all through the economic system we will find that not only has the distribution of resources, for instance, land use and the use of the labor, been altered in many different areas, but the distribution of income has also been altered in favor of the wheat producers and some others. The distribution of income as between rich and poor will have been altered, that is, the equality or inequality of incomes will have changed unless the distribution of incomes by size among the wheat producers is exactly the same as it is in the rest of society, which is most unlikely. Furthermore, even the distribution of assets among owners will have been altered, as land which is peculiarly suitable for growing wheat will have risen in value relative to other land. The producers of wheat-growing machinery will have received at least a temporary windfall and increased their assets, and this again will produce many repercussions around the system. Thus even in a pure exchange economy, changes in the price structure will affect not only who *does* what, when, and where, but also who *gets* what, when, and where.

Similarly, if we take the grants economy or the transfer economy as something which is peculiarly political, as over and against the exchange section which is more strictly economic, we find that it is impossible to make a grant or even to collect a tax without changing both the allocation of resources and the distribution of income and assets. Thus, suppose the Ford Foundation or even the National Science Foundation makes a big grant for research in medicine. This will alter the allocation of resources in favor of the field in which the grant is given and away from other fields. It will also alter the distribution of income, raising the income of medical researchers relative to others. The fabric of society indeed is such a closely woven network that it is almost impossible to do anything anywhere which does not affect everything everywhere. The plain fact is that decisions are not fractionalized into "economic" decisions which allocate resources and "political" decisions which distribute the result. All decisions have mixed effects so we cannot classify them according to their consequences. At this point it would seem that both allocation and distribution are firmly part of a single science called political economy!

Nevertheless, the distinction between the political and the economic aspect of the social system is talked about so much that we must try and search further for some reason for it. We may find ourselves on more secure ground then, if we focus on the distinction between *individual* action and decision and *collective* action and decision with the first being more the province of the economists and the second more the province of the political scientists. All social dynamics arise out of some sort of discontent. If we are completely happy about today we will simply try to reproduce it tomorrow, and the social system will be in equilibrium. It is only as we contemplate the present with disfavor that we are likely to see a future which is different from it.

Discontent, however, can take two rather different forms—personal or political. People seek to relieve personal discontent by operating within the perceived system of personal opportunities. Personal discontent with a marriage leads a man to get a divorce rather than to reform the marriage laws. Personal discontent with a location drives a man to migrate, rather than to press for urban renewal. Personal discontent with existing income drives a man to try new occupations or to go to night school and improve his capacity or even to marry a rich wife, rather than to agitate for a war on poverty. This is the sort of activity which is contemplated in the pure economic model of an exchange economy in which people's constant desire to better themselves as individuals, or at least as members of families, drives them into new occupations, new enterprises, and new investments and leads to the division of labor, and increased productivity for the ultimate benefit of all. This, of course, is Adam

Smith's "invisible hand," which turns the dross of private selfishness and the attempt to allay private discontent into the gold of public good. This is the source of the famous "principle of equal advantage," which states that if the total advantages of different occupations of either labor or capital are unequal, resources will tend to move from the occupations of less advantage into the occupations of greater advantage, thereby increasing the advantages of the less advantageous occupations and diminishing the advantages of the more advantageous occupations, the movement only ceasing when all occupations are equally advantageous. In fact, of course, the movement continues all the time as underlying conditions continuously change.

Political discontent, by contrast, is reflected not in action designed to find a better niche for the individual in the existing system, but in action designed to change the system itself. Political discontent then is reflected in activity such as joining a political party, engaging in propaganda and agitation, voting in elections, and, in the extreme case, taking up arms in civil war or a bloody revolution. One very important question regarding which we have surprisingly little evidence is what precisely it is in the social situation or perhaps in the character of the individual which moves him to the expression of either personal discontent or political discontent, for these, while not necessarily rigid alternatives in that one person may follow both patterns at the same time, certainly tend to be more competitive than complementary. That is to say, the person who is strongly motivated by a desire to better his own condition within the existing framework of society is not likely to be a revolutionary or even a very active political type. Therefore, he will, quite rightly, see political activity of any kind as a distraction and a detriment to his personal ambitions, except in the somewhat rare case in which the road to personal advancement is perceived as going through the acquisition of political influence and power.

By contrast, the person who is seething with political discontent —the revolutionary, the alienated, the dissident, whether of left or right—is apt to be either a middle-aged person who has failed in the satisfaction of his personal discontent and become stuck in a location, an occupation, or even a marriage from which he cannot escape and which he finds undesirable, or a young person who has found the competitive "rat race" of the educational and economic establishment too much for him and has decided that he will get more satisfaction out of trying to change the system. It is at least a plausible hypothesis that in social situations where personal discontent is frequently frustrated, economic development is slow, and there are rigid class structures and caste structures that prohibit upward mobility, discontent is more likely to take a political form. On the other hand, it is also true that in rigid and oppressive societies in which political discontent is brutally suppressed and the chances of political change seem poor people get discouraged from political action and tend to express their discontent in private mobility.

Political systems vary enormously ranging from sheer despotisms and tyrannies which rely on an almost pure threat system to democratic societies in which the threat system is at least muted and limited by constitutional and other restraints. The latter political systems are much more capable of being described in economic terms than the former. In recent years a number of authors have applied economic ways of thinking, suitably modified, to the political environment with considerable success. Lindblom and Dahl,[1] as noted earlier, have a concept which they call "disjointed incrementalism" which they use in the explanation of the bureaucratic and political decision-making process, the idea being essentially that a gap is perceived between some perceived reality and some ideal situation and steps are taken to close this gap. Closing one gap, however, always opens others; solving one problem creates others, and then these in turn are perceived as problems and an attempt is made to close the gaps between ideals and reality in these other cases. This process can ramify almost indefinitely and it is by no means demonstrated that

[1] Robert Dahl and Charles E. Lindblom, *Politics, Economics and Welfare,* Harper, New York, 1953.

it cannot run into what I have called "perverse dynamics," in which case everybody becomes worse off. Nevertheless, there are many situations in which this process is reasonably successful and develops an overall pattern of problem solving in society; a kind of political invisible hand which sees to it that large problems, which no single person could grasp, still less solve, are solved in fact by many persons in small increments.

One important problem here, which has by no means been solved, is that of spelling out the conditions under which processes of disjointed incrementalism lead to general betterment and the conditions under which they lead to perverse dynamics and a general worsening of the situation. The latter development is most likely to take place under conditions of malevolence and deterrence. This is the sort of thing which gives us an arms race, for instance. One country perceives that it is insecure relative to another country or to potential combinations of countries and hence it increases its "war industry" and its arms budget. This creates problems for the other countries, making them feel less secure, so they likewise increase their war budgets. This recreates insecurity in the first country, which increases its war budget still further, and an arms race is on. Processes of this kind always lead away from the "Paretian optimum," which we shall examine later, in the sense that they lead to positions where everybody is worse off. On the other hand, one sees the processes of disjointed incrementalism operate fairly successfully in universities, in corporations, and indeed in organizations of many kinds, and the "invisible hand" of Adam Smith is of course the prize example of disjointed incrementalism in society as a whole operating to produce a general process of amelioration and development. It may well be that the critical variable which divides benign processes of this kind, which make everybody better off, from the malign ones, which makes everybody worse off, is whether the incremental decision is one which takes advantage of some kind of opportunity for increasing productivity. A move by one individual toward what is for him a better situation or even the solving of a problem by one bureaucrat may make other individuals or other problem solvers worse off. If the move involves pure redistribution, as in the case of the bandit, and still more if it is a move in a negative-sum game in which one person becomes better off at the expense of another person who suffers a more than proportionate loss, the process is likely to be malign. Where, however, dissatisfactions and discontents have the effect of increasing the productivity of the discontented, the improvement in the latter's position may not result in a worsening of anybody else's position, in which case a general gain is the result.

This principle suggests that political processes under conditions of general economic development may be very different from political processes in a stagnant economy and decidedly different from political processes in a declining one. In a stagnant economy a gain by one person almost has to be achieved at the cost of a loss by another. Under these circumstances even personal betterment is perceived as a political struggle, for the person who moves to a better opportunity in effect pushes somebody else down to a worse one. Political conflict in such a society is so acute that it may only be resolved by an extreme authoritarian dictatorship or monarchy, and reliance on a brutal threat system. In a society which is enjoying rapid economic development, however, the political situation is much easier. If A gets more, B does not necessarily get less. In fact B may get more too. There may be political quarrels over the sharing of the increase but these are likely to be much less acute and desperate than quarrels over the sharing of a stagnant or diminishing total. In a stationary society politics is a game of "beggar my neighbor"; in a developing society it is a game of benefiting my neighbor not quite so much as I am benefiting, which is a game which is much less likely to arouse intense emotions.

The relationships between liberalism, democracy, toleration, and other political virtues and economic development are extremely complex, but very important. The relationships are highly reciprocal but not always stable. There are many cases where the establishment of formal democratic institutions in a society which did not have the spirit or the culture to make them workable has actually inhibited development. A great many Latin American countries are sad cases in point. It is also true that occasionally authoritarian and dictatorial regimes have been able to impose economic development on a people who were rather unwilling, unwilling, that is, to pay the present costs without considerable political repression. On the other hand, regimes that are too authoritarian and too tyrannical have to divert so many of their resources into the suppression of discontent, and are so little subject to the correction of policy mistakes, that they are apt to make disastrous mistakes in economic policy and planning, and set back development thereby. The record of Stalin in the Soviet Union and Mao Tse Tung's record in China are examples of this proposition. Certainly in its origins the great developmental process of the last two or three hundred years was closely associated with the development of tolerant but also rather secure political regimes, such as that which came into being in England after the Glorious Revolution of 1688; of course, in the United States liberal democracy and economic development have gone hand in hand almost from the beginning. A very important question to which it is perhaps too soon to give an asnwer is whether economic development itself, when it is successful, will result in the liberalization of a political regime. There are certainly signs of this in the socialist camp though it is perhaps a little too early to say how far the movement will go. In Czechoslovakia indeed the movement for liberalization seems to have been motivated mainly by discontent with the economic failures of a relatively repressive and authoritarian regime.

Another field where economic concepts have had some contribution to make to the understanding of political institutions is in voting behavior and party policies in a democracy with the party system. The parallel has often been drawn between a vote in an election and the dollar which a consumer or householder spends on one thing or another. In a market-type economy the allocation of resources among different employments and industries is very largely determined by the "dollar votes" of households and investors. Firms which produce things that people are willing to vote for, or purchase, will thrive, while those which produce things which people are disinclined to vote for, that is, buy, will languish or even become extinct. Similarly, it is argued that a political party that wants to get its candidates elected and assume political power must obtain a majority of the votes in an election. This means essentially that it must offer a "product" in the mind of the electorate which will attract the larger number of votes.

We must be careful, however, not to draw the parallels too sharply. In the market there are in effect a very large number of parties, there is no majority rule, and there is the possibility of a wide diversity of mixtures of commodity purchases and a wide diversity in styles of life. In the political area, where majority rule is the convention, diversity can only be achieved through coalitions offering packages, one of which will appeal to more voters than the others. It is as if in economic life we had only two firms, each of them offering a complete package of consumer goods in relatively fixed proportions, so that in effect we had a choice between two enormous packages of commodities and could not make our own selection. This, however, is precisely the difference between public goods and private goods; the public goods which are offered through the political process come in large heterogeneous packages. We are still a long way from solving the problem of the political expression of individual demands. Up to now, for instance, we have not even dared to allow the individual to specify what his taxes may be used for, except in the case of local taxes for specific purposes, such as school taxes or sewer and water taxes. The idea that the federal taxpayer should have any voice at all in deciding what the federal budget should be would cause politicians to turn pale with fright. Unless this much is granted, however, the parallel between the vote and the purchase breaks down.

A problem of great interest and importance, which has been raised by Galbraith,[2] is how far the consumer or household in the case of the market, or the voter in the case of the political process, actually calls the tune and determines what shall be produced and how far the seller or producer in the case of the market, or the political apparatus in the case of the state, decides autonomously what it wants to do and then "sells" its product to the consumer or voter. It is pretty clear that both of these processes are at work in both economic and political life. What Galbraith calls the "accepted sequence," in which for instance the consumer decides that he wants hula hoops and producers snap to attention and produce them in sufficient quantity to satisfy the demand at profitable prices, is in fact something which does take place over large areas of life, as a great many producers have discovered to their cost or gain. Similarly, politicians or political parties which get involved in unpopular wars or get blamed for depressions soon find out that the accepted sequence operates even in politics and the voter cannot be pushed beyond a certain point.

It is true, however, that what Galbraith calls the "revised sequence" also operates. The persuasive resources of Madison Avenue and their political equivalent in the shape of the lobbyist and the persuasive politician come into play to sell the customer or the voter something which he may not really want and would not demand if left to his own devices. The very existence of a large advertising industry suggests that this revised sequence does in fact operate over part of the market economy. There is no doubt that it also operates in political life. For instance, there was no real grass roots demand for social security, even after the Great Depression. A group of able and socially minded intellectuals decided that this was what the country needed and in effect sold it to the politicians and later to the electorate. Similarly, it would be hard to maintain that there was a large grass roots demand for a war in Vietnam with President Johnson reluctantly producing a supply.

[2] J. K. Galbraith, *The New Industrial State,* Houghton Mifflin, Boston, 1967.

Nevertheless, there are many examples of the revised sequence breaking down, one being the famous case of the Edsel. In political life, the war in Vietnam seems to be an "Edsel," and all the efforts to sell it are not being very successful. The power of the producer and the politician, however, is still very substantial, and we must not underestimate the fact that an agency like the Department of Defense has almost one lobbyist for every congressman and has sold national greatness and militarism at least as effectively as Madison Avenue has sold detergents and deodorants. Between the two of them they could probably purify the hands even of Lady Macbeth.

One point at which economics has traditionally impinged on the political structure has been in the matter of giving good advice to the Sovereign. Economists have rarely eschewed this activity even though they have frequently preached themselves sermons against it. Insofar, however, as one of the main standards of success of governmental authority is the promotion of economic well-being, economists certainly have as good a right as anybody to give advice to the Sovereign. On the whole there have been two schools of advice givers which might be described as the "tight" and the "loose." The tight school is characterized particularly by what is known as welfare economics. This is a body of theory which, incidentally, has practically nothing to do with welfare as the term is often understood in ordinary political discourse. It is an attempt to answer with great exactness the question, what do we as economists really mean when we say that one state or condition of the social system is economically "better" than another? This is a good question, even if at the end of fifty years of discussion the answer that emerges is that we are not really sure. This at least is a good honest conclusion and the exercise that we have gone through as economists to reach it is one that other social scientists might well emulate. Out of welfare economics indeed has come a very important concept which we call the Paretian optimum and a set of economic road signs, as it were, that convey about the same type of information to the policy maker that "sharp curve," "steep hill," and "falling rocks" do to the motorist.

The Paretian optimum can perhaps best be understood in the negative sense. A society is *not* at a Paretian optimum if it can move to another position or state in which even one person is better off in his own estimation and no person is worse off in his own estimation. There is of course an implicit assumption here that if we are not at a Paretian optimum moving toward it is a good thing. This involves large ethical assumptions, especially about the absence of malevolence, of which economists are not always aware. Nevertheless, it is a nice, decent, humane principle, and when political questions are put in this way political conflict can hardly fail to become more sweet and reasonable. A corollary of the Paretian optimum is the compensation principle, which says that even a movement toward a state in which some people are worse off may be turned into a movement toward the optimum, that is, a movement toward improvement, if the people who are better off can compensate the people who are worse off and still be better off themselves than they were originally. The whole idea of compensation as a political ideal indeed is something which, one suspects, creeps into political life from economics. The idea that it is often better to buy somebody off than to knock him down is a thoroughly economic idea. It does not appeal much to men of principle, moralists, and revolutionaries, but it very probably adds to human happiness and diminishes human misery. This is not a bad accomplishment.

The "road signs" which welfare economics produces relate mainly to the dangers of intervening unskillfully in the system of relative prices. If people are not allowed to trade freely with each other, if, for instance, there are quantitative restrictions, quotas, licensing, and so forth, opportunities for gain through trade are lost, and this is a real cost to society. This does not mean of course that restrictions and regulations are never justified. For instance most welfare economists would agree that interference with slavery or even prostitution may be justified. A road sign is a warning rather than a prohibition, and indeed one of the road signs is a warning against prohibitions. When one sees furthermore the extraordinary handicaps that some countries have imposed on themselves in the name of economic planning because they have not paid attention to the road signs of the welfare economists, one at least gets the feeling that they are worth paying some attention to, even though they do not provide a complete guide for action, and indeed are not intended to provide such.

Although welfare economics provides certain warning signs, it does not tell us which road we ought to go on, and it is perhaps too modest and self-abasing when it comes to some possible contributions toward political problems which involve what economists call interpersonal comparisons of utility. Interpersonal comparison means that if A is better off and B is worse off, we should be able to say whether the advantage to A outweighs the disadvantage to B, even if we cannot compensate. There are many political decisions, which have to be made, which do in fact involve interpersonal comparisons. It is absurd to say that we cannot make interpersonal comparisons when in fact we do. Indeed the Paretian optimum itself involves interpersonal comparisons of a kind in the sense that it makes what is essentially a value judgment when it implies that no person should be worse off. Unfortunately, in political life there is a good deal of malevolence, and many decisions are made with the express object of making some person worse off. Without interpersonal comparisons indeed the whole apparatus of criminal law and the courts, the whole concept of punishment, and certainly the whole concept of war would simply fall to the ground. One might argue indeed that this would be a good thing. Nevertheless, the political realities of the moment would not admit this. Hence in political decision making the Paretian principle is not enough.

In this regard what is sometimes called the "older" welfare economics, which is the economics of people like Pigou,[3] has something

[3] A. C. Pigou, *The Economics of Welfare*, Macmillan, London, 1932.

to recommend it. Pigou assumed in effect that we could, theoretically at least, have some objective criterion of human welfare and that the total welfare of society would be maximized at the point where the additional welfare due to an additional dollar would be the same for all people, for if transferring a dollar from A to B increased B's welfare more than it diminished A's welfare then the total quantity of welfare would increase. The idea of a total quantity of welfare is certainly not absurd, even though there may be insuperable difficulties in the way of an objective measurement. As interpersonal comparisons are in fact made through a political process, in many respects the older welfare economics is more applicable to politics than the more elegant welfare economics of the modern school. It has the important implication for instance that equality of income does not maximize welfare unless all people are alike in their capacity for the enjoyment of income. If in fact some people enjoy income more than others, those who enjoy income the most and enjoy being rich the most should be rich, or at least should be richer than those who do not enjoy being rich. This is a somewhat treacherous argument which can be used, if we are not careful, to justify privilege of all kinds in both socialist and capitalist societies, but it is at least an argument which cannot be ruled out as nonsensical and an argument that reflects a real political problem. What for instance is the ideal rate of progression for an income tax? This is a question that economists have denied that they could answer but which Congress has had to decide; the problem is an economic one even if the answer is political.

The "loose" school of policy advisers consists of those who give general advice on the objectives of economic policy and come up with a certain set of road signs pointing out the dangers and the kind of mistakes which may be made. There is indeed a pretty fair consensus about the larger objectives of economic policy. We almost all agree that in successful societies at the present time there should at least be a positive rate of economic growth even though we do not agree as to what the optimum rate of growth may be. Politically the problem of the optimum rate of growth is important. A society can grow too fast and at too great a cost, either in terms of the burden placed on its present generation, especially its present generation of young people or in terms of its ultimate stability and capacity to provide a good life. Some countries, indeed, such as Burma have decided that economic growth is too disruptive to their society, at least in its present state and have virtually decided not to grow at all in the interest of national stability and out of fear of putting too great a strain on the social framework. It would be a rash economist who would deny a society the right to make this decision. Nevertheless, there still remains a very broad consensus in both capitalist and socialist countries that rates of growth of the order at least of 5 percent are desirable for most countries, while a rate of growth of zero is undesirable and a negative rate of growth, extremely undesirable. There is also a pretty wide consensus that growth should be reasonably stable, that is, it is undesirable to alternate periods of very rapid growth with periods of stagnation, decline, or unemployment. There is widespread agreement, for instance, that unemployment above a certain figure, say 3 or 4 percent of the labor force, is very undesirable; an unemployment figure of 10 percent is regarded as extremely undesirable and an indication of a basic failure in economic policy.

Other objectives of economic policy which might be described as justice and freedom are much harder to define but are still important in political rhetoric and in passing judgment on the failure or success of a regime. For instance, a society which has a rapid rate of growth, but one in which all growth is concentrated in a small sector or among a certain class or caste or race within the society would be regarded by most people as highly unsatisfactory for there is widespread agreement that the benefits of economic growth should be widely diffused, even if the people who are ultimately responsible for that growth represent only a small percentage of the population.

On the matter of what constitutes economic justice, there is much less consensus than there is on the general desirability of growth. In the United States, for instance, should we view with alarm the constantly rising proportion of the national income which goes to interest on the grounds that this represents a burden on society which should be minimized? What would be the ideal, or at least a generally acceptable, division of the national income between labor income and property income? These are the kinds of questions that economists on the whole have not felt competent to answer. When we come to the concept of economic freedom there is even less consensus. Some people feel that it is extremely important for the economic system to have free markets, freedom of exchange, free capital markets, and so on, whereas others, especially of course in the socialist countries, feel that these freedoms are undesirable and should be eliminated, no doubt in the interest of some larger freedom, whatever that may be. The problem of freedom is closely related to the problem of what is regarded as legitimate. This is a very large and difficult subject. We might say therefore that while the "tight" school of economic advisers has a strong consensus about things which perhaps do not matter very much politically, the "loose" school suffers from a considerable lack of consensus but in spite of this may be able to give a great deal of useful advice. We may indeed think of general economic welfare as a kind of "mesa" rather than a sharp peak in that there is a large area of tableland with a great variety of positions the society can assume, all of which are about equally good. The search for the highest point on the tableland is probably fruitless. On the other hand, a mesa has cliffs and it may be one of the principal businesses of economics in regard to giving good advice to the politician to warn him where the cliffs are and where disaster may ensue.

If economics can set up a system of distant early warning signs for social cliffs, it will be abundantly justified politically. Major depressions are certainly one of these cliffs, and we have developed pretty fair devices now for warning and for turning away. There are probably other cliffs of which we are not so well aware, such as, for instance, the problems involved in the transmission of the culture of a society from one generation to the next, the problems involved in legitimacy and political stability, and so on about which economists have not had very much to say. Perhaps our biggest success to date is in dealing with the problem of unemployment and the avoidance of major depression, and our biggest failure is in dealing with the problem of self-perpetuating poverty cultures, whether in the poor countries or in the ghettos of our cities. This latter problem, however, is perhaps beyond the real competence of the economist as such and demands an integrated social science.

FIVE

Economics as a Mathematical Science

It is almost as hard to define mathematics as it is to define economics, and one is tempted to fall back on the famous old definition attributed to Jacob Viner, "Economics is what economists do," and say that mathematics is what mathematicians do. A large part of mathematics deals with the formal relations of quantities or numbers. This, however, by no means exhausts the field for a great deal of modern mathematics consists of the study of the formal relationships of structures. Also, it is hard to tell, especially in these days, where logic leaves off and mathematics begins; indeed, it can be argued that they are simply parts of a single discipline.

If there is a single concept which unifies all of mathematics, it is the concept of moving to progressively higher levels of abstraction in a way that permits the detection of formal inconsistencies and incongruities. As the unforgivable sin of the scientific community is telling lies, the unforgivable sin among mathematicians is the failure to perceive inconsistencies in a system at the appropriate level of abstraction. One has to put in the last phrase because inconsistencies at one level of abstraction may not be inconsistencies at another. Just how mathematicians agree as to what inconsistencies are compatible with what level of abstraction is something of a puzzle. The degree of agreement among mathematicians is extraordinarily high. Mathematics is the one subculture where the ability to resolve conflicts by applying formal principles seems to be almost one hundred percent. I am not sure that we understand completely why this is so.

Mathematics has played a crucial role in the growth of human knowledge and especially in the growth of scientific knowledge. There are several reasons for this. In the first place mathematics has developed a universal language of abstract symbols which is virtually incapable of ambiguity. When one mathematician follows the argument of another, we have a great deal of confidence that what was in the mind of the writer is transferred almost without loss to the mind of the reader. In ordinary language there is a great deal of slack in the sense that what is in the mind of the speaker or writer may not be reproduced at all in the mind of the hearer or reader, who introduces the communication into his own image through his own information filter. This is because words are used in many different contexts and retain something of the meaning of all the contexts in which they are used. It is these "overtones" of meaning which give language, and especially poetry, its richness and much of its power to give pleasure. But this very richness of meaning is an obstacle when it comes to the undistorted transfer of images from one mind to another. A great poem will have a different impact on every mind that it touches; this, indeed, is why it is great. This is also why poetry is an unsuitable medium for the transfer of exact images. At the mathematical level of abstraction there is very little dispute about the meaning of symbols. For instance x^2 means something multiplied by itself in any language, and it means nothing else.

Another virtue of mathematical language noted already is that it is remarkably successful in revealing inconsistencies. Hence it is capable of producing formal models of the world, the inferences from which cannot be denied. This is of great importance in the process of human learning. If we think of learning as essentially a process by which error is detected and eliminated in our image of the world, that is, in our internal view of the world, then, as Hume pointed out long ago, there is no way of comparing an image with the corresponding reality, for we can only compare images with images. There is, however, what can be called a learning process by which the image comes to approximate reality through the process of detection and rejection of error. Error is detected when there is a disappointment, that is, when some image of the future is not fulfilled. Disappointment in itself, however, is not enough to produce knowledge, because there is the further task of detecting where the error lies. In "folk knowledge," that is, the ordinary knowledge which we acquire in common life, inferences and expectations are vague enough so that disappointment often results in our rejecting the inference rather than revising our image of the world. It is a great virtue of mathematics that its capacity for internal consistency prevents the rejection of inferences which are based on it. Therefore if we make predictions which are based on a mathematical model and these are disappointed, we are virtually forced to revise our model. We cannot simply brush off the disappointment as a failure of inference, though it may still be interpreted as a failure of observation.

Images of the world can only take the form of mathematical models if the world itself has orderly patterns which mathematical models can describe. A world without such patterns indeed is present in our imaginations in fantasy, fairy stories, and magic. This is a world in which literally there are no physical constants. It is a world of flying carpets, magic wands, wishing caps, and so on. It is probably just as well for us that we do not live in this world of fantasy but in a world in which there are physical constants and indeed biological and social constants. We soon learn at the subconscious level as we grow up that there is a gravitational constant. We learn that if we fall we shall be hurt, that we cannot jump very high, that there are limits as to how far we can throw a ball, and so on. A tennis player operates with a considerable number of physical constants which he "knows" unconsciously. It is the great task of science to bring these dimly-perceived systems into the full consciousness of man, in other words, to identify the constants and the relationships which they determine. In this task mathematics has an essential role, that of the development of models of successive degrees of approximation.

Thus the theory of a falling body starts with the first approximation of a gravitational constant which produces—and is measured by—constant acceleration. This constant acceleration is the gravitational constant, which is 32 feet, or 9.81 meters, per second per second. From this we can easily derive the velocity of a falling body at any time and the distance which it has fallen. For bodies which are heavy in relation to their area this formula can be tested and works very well. For bodies which are light in relation to their area, like leaves and snowflakes, it does not work at all, and we have to introduce a new approximation involving air resistance. This illustrates incidentally a fact which was called to my attention by Anatol Rapoport, namely, that the mere empirical study of all falling bodies would never have given us the law of gravitation, for most of them, such as leaves, snowflakes, and so on, apparently do not obey this law, and it would have been very hard to find the first approximation of constant acceleration if we had not been able to drop cannonballs in the air or lighter things in a vacuum. This again perhaps illustrates in a subtle way the importance of mathematics. For the poet a falling leaf is a simple thing in itself, however complex the emotions which it may evoke. For the mathematician it is appallingly complicated; even today it is probably beyond his reach to describe its dynamics explicitly. Mathematics therefore simply by its inadequacies forces us into simplicity, which is almost the same as saying that it forces us into first approximations on the solid basis of which we can erect second, third, and further approximations. In this way it saves us from pure empiricism which merely observes, records, and classifies on the basis of superficial similarities. Biology is still not completely liberated from a system of purely empirical and observational taxonomy or classification.

In the social sciences, and especially in economics, the use of mathematics likewise forces us into simplicity. This is both its power and its danger. Abstractions are not realities, the world is complex not simple, and there is a real danger that we shall become so enamored of mathematical models with their simplicities that we think the world is actually like them. This danger was present in formal economics even before mathematics was introduced. The classical economists developed powerful abstract images of the economic system which were mathematical in substance though expressed in literary form. Perhaps because of the literary power and elegance of the language in which these models were expressed, they acquired a hold over the minds of men which has sometimes prevented them from being refined into closer approximations of reality. Here perhaps the puritanism of mathematics, its inability as a language to develop richness, color, and innuendo will tend to keep people from being overimpressed with models of the world that are satisfying but at the same time inaccurate. There is a danger on the other side however that the use of mathematics with its attendant arts of inference and manipulation may lead to a loss of interest in the real world, and this again can be a powerful obstacle to the advance of knowledge. There is a story that has been going around about a physicist, a chemist, and an economist who were stranded on a desert island with no implements and a can of food. The physicist and the chemist each devised an ingenious mechanism for getting the can open; the economist merely said, "Assume we have a can opener"! All mathematics begins with assumptions, and in the applied fields it is all too easy to start with assumptions that are not so and then proceed from these assumptions to a chain of reasoning so intricate that the conclusions at which we arrive derive persuasiveness from the reasoning alone and we forget that no chain of argument can come closer to the truth than its assumptions.

With this background in mind therefore let us take a look at some of the more important applications of mathematics to economics. Let us take first the concept of an equilibrium system as the solution of a set of simultaneous equations. We have already run into this concept in Chapter 2, in considering the equilibrium of ecological systems. It is interesting to see how many rungs we can climb in the ladder of abstraction. We start off with objects in the real world—cups and saucers, pigs, bananas, etc. The first abstraction is the concept of number itself; we notice that two pigs and two bananas or two anything have something in common, so we get the idea of "two-ness" as something divorced from the actual objects. The next step in abstraction is the concept of a relation. We notice that certain things go together. We expect to find a saucer under our cup, Dick goes with Jane, and so on. The same can be true of numbers—we get the idea of an ordered pair, such as (4, 6). A husband and a wife are a pair, but if a husband always precedes the wife, they are an ordered pair. There are, of course, an infinite number of ordered pairs. If we can define a set of them in such a way that some ordered pairs are members of the set and some are not, we have a relation, though relations that are very inclusive are not very interesting. One of the most interesting relations is the "function," which is a set of ordered pairs such that if one member of the pair is specified, then there is only one, or at best there are very few, numbers which can represent the other member of the pair. Thus a crowd of married couples are a function; for every husband one can identify one and only one lady who is his wife. In numerical terms consider a set of ordered pairs as follows: (0,3), (1,5), (2,7), (3,9), (4,11), and so on. We can easily spot that there is a rule here, and if we know the rule and if we are given one of the numbers in a pair, we can predict the other. Given this rule we can write down an indefinite number of pairs which conform to the rule. In the above case if x is the first member of the pair and y is the second member, the rule can be written $y = 3 + 2x$, as the reader may test for himself.

Suppose now that we have another set of ordered pairs as follows: (0,12), (1,11), (2,10), (3,9), (4,8), etc. If we compare this set with the first set, we see that they have one and only one ordered pair in common, namely (3,9). Whenever a set of rules applied together eliminates all but one or at most a few ordered pairs, we say this is a "solution." If there is only one ordered pair which satisfies a set of rules we say this is a "unique solution."

The reader who has had a course in elementary economics will immediately recognize the above functions as fairly typical of supply and demand functions and the solution as an equilibrium price or quantity. If we suppose the first member of each of the ordered pairs in the first set to be the quantity of a commodity supplied and the second member to be the price, we see that unless the price is greater than 3 nothing will be supplied; if the price is 5, 1 unit will be supplied; if the price 7, 2 units will be supplied, and so on as we go to higher prices. Similarly, the second function can easily represent a demand function where the first figure in each pair represents the quantity demanded and the second the corresponding price. Here with a price as high as 12, nothing will be bought; at a price of 11, 1 unit will be bought; at a price of 10, 2 units will be bought, and so on. The solution here represents an equilibrium because we suppose as the condition of equilibrium that the quantity offered for sale equal the quantity purchased. The only ordered pair which will fulfill this condition of satisfying both functions is (3,9), suggesting that at a price of 9, 3 units will be offered and 3 units will be purchased. If we wanted to express this in general terms we would write three equations where p is the price, q_s is the quantity offered for sale, and q_d the quantity offered to purchase, as follow:

$$q_s = F_s\,(p)$$
$$q_d = F_d\,(p)$$
$$q_s = q_d$$

The third equation here is the condition of equilibrium. The "*F*" in the other equations simply stands for function and can be read as "depends upon" so we can read the first equation, "the quantity supplied depends upon the price"; the second, "the quantity demanded depends upon the price"; and the third equation, "the price will tend to be that at which the quantity demanded equals the quantity supplied." The reader may ask, why do we have to express all this in mathematical language? The answer is that we do not; Adam Smith in fact expressed the same thing in very beautiful English. The great advantage of mathematical language, however, is that it becomes easy to generalize the kind of relationships and conditions of equilibrium and assumptions which are involved to include large numbers of variables, something which it is very hard to do in ordinary language. Thus, we can leap immediately from the ordered pair to the ordered triplet (x,y,z), which defines functions of three variables, and then to the "n-tuplet" of any number of variables, and we can see that the basic principles still apply. What is even more important, we occasionally find that simple models do *not* apply when they are generalized.

Thus, we can easily generalize the simple equations of demand and supply and suppose that the quantities demanded and supplied of each commodity are functions of *all* prices. If there are n commodities this given us $3n$ variables; n prices, n quantities demanded, and n quantities supplied. We also have $3n$ equations; n for the quantity demanded, n for the quantity supplied, and n equations of equilibrium showing that each quantity demanded is equal to the quantity supplied. If in any system the number of equations is equal to the number of unknowns, a solution is possible though it does not necessarily exist in real numbers, still less in positive numbers, nor need it be unique. A model of *n* equations and *n* unknowns can be expanded as far as we like as long as for every additional variable we add an additional equation. We should be careful here however of what might be called mathematical formalism. It is not satisfactory simply to postulate an equilibrium with *n* equations with *n* unknowns if we do not know more about the system than this. We cannot know whether the equilibrium is stable, for instance, unless we know something about the dynamics of the system, and we cannot know whether the solution is in real numbers or whether it is unique unless we can specify certain things about the. nature of the functions. The exact specification of the system therefore is very far from complete when we simply identify a number of equations and a corresponding number of unknowns. Economists in the past at least have been prone to leave it at that without further investigation.

The principal value of equilibrium analysis lies in what is called comparative statics. This consists of asking ourselves in an equilibrium system how the position of equilibrium will change if the parameters of the system change. In quantitative terms this is known as sensitivity analysis. A system is *sensitive* if the position of equilibrium changes a great deal when the parameters change a little. It is important to know when systems in the real world are sensitive, since a sensitive system has a capacity for going very badly wrong with quite small changes in circumstances, though it also has the capacity of being very easily brought back on course by relatively small adjustments. Thus, in the simple case of an equilibrium of demand and supply, if the demand curve has a negative slope and the supply curve has a positive slope, the system will be fairly insensitive to changes in the demand and supply functions themselves. If, however, the demand and supply curves are similar with similar slopes then quite small changes in the functions can produce a large change in the position of equilibrium. This is illustrated in Figure 5-1. *DD* is an initial demand curve, *SS* a positive slope supply curve, and *E*, the point of equilibrium. A shift in the demand curve to

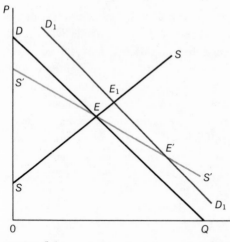

FIGURE 5-1

D_1D_1 will shift the equilibrium to E_1. If however the supply curve had been negatively sloped, like $S'S'$, the shift in the demand curve would have moved the equilibrium to E'—a much larger move.

Another important use of mathematics in economics has been in what is called the "theory of maximizing behavior." The theory of economic behavior indeed, as we have already examined it in Chapter 3, can be described as a set of elaborate mathematical variations on the theme that everyone does what he thinks is best at the time. The concept of "best" however implies either a set of cardinal numbers, one of which is larger than any of the others, or a set of ordinal numbers, one of which is "first" or superior to all the others. Whenever we have such a set the mathematical theory of maximization or minimization may turn out to be relevant. Where we have continuous functions differential calculus can be employed to define points in a system where some "maximand" is maximized; the maximand is that variable which measures "goodness" so when it is maximized we have the "best" situation. The application of differential calculus to these problems leads to what is called "marginal analysis," marginal "x" being the literary term for a differential coefficient, which may be defined roughly as the increase in one variable (n) which results from a very small unit increase in another. The problem of maximization is how to find the "top" of a "mountain," the height of which is the maximand. At the top of a mountain, however, we are neither going up nor going down, that is, the marginal quantities involving the maximand are all zero. This is the fundamental principle of marginal analysis.

We have to be careful here also of mathematical formalism, especially where there may be a number of maximum positions. When the maximand function is noncontinuous, or where it exhibits a number of maxima, marginal analysis breaks down, and we have to fall back on something called programming, which is however only another set of operations for finding a maximum. Programming has actually turned out to be more useful in practice than the application of differential calculus, which frequently faces a severe information problem and easily lapses into mathematical formalism. There is no point in telling the businessman that he should equate marginal cost with marginal revenue if he has no way of finding out in the course of his decision-making process what these quantities are. Programming, whether linear or nonlinear, is essentially a "program" for finding out which way is "up," that is, for locating the maximand, as we move from one point to another in a complicated system. If we move "up" a sufficient number of times we will presumably eventually reach the top.

In many systems however the top when we get there may not consist of a unique peak but may consist of a "plateau" of a large number of equally good positions. In many respects this corresponds to the real social system where we are faced with "mesas" rather than mountain peaks and where it does not matter very much where we are in the system as long as we do not fall over the edge. Maximization theory is not much use at this point, as it may not help us at all in detecting where the "cliffs" of a system are. An alternative theory of economic behavior put forth by Herbert Simon is known as "sat-isficing." Essentially it involves slicing the tops off our maximand mountains and turning them into mesas so that as long as we are above a certain point anything will do, and we will be satisfied and hence will not try to change the position.

The definition of the maximand itself often raises great difficul-ties. Formally the maximand may be defined as "utility," utility sim-ply being what goes up when things are better. Utility theory how-ever easily lapses into mathematical formalism. Unless we can say something about the nature of the utility function, we fall into the trap of supposing that all behavior increases utility and therefore a critique of economic behavior is impossible. The attempt to find "objective" maximands is perhaps more rewarding though even here the difficulties are very great. In the elementary theory of the firm, for instance, it is often supposed that firms maximize profits; nobody supposes, however, that this is any more than a first approximation be-cause all firms will be prepared to sacrifice profits for something, in which case they are not really maximized. Furthermore, it is not easy to agree about what the measure of profits should be, whether, for instance, it should be some sort of rate of return on capital, ex-pressed as a percent per annum, whether it should be some capital-ized value of the enterprise, or whether it should be some measure of income.

The difficulties expand rapidly as we try to introduce the concept of economic decision making under uncertainty. Here indeed it may be the fear of loss rather than the hope of gain which ulti-mately sets the limits on behavior. We may, for instance, minimize regrets rather than maximize expected value. The whole subject of rational behavior under uncertainty indeed is one of great difficulty. Game theory has succeeded in formalizing some of the problems and suggesting certain solutions such as the "minimax," which may be verbalized as "act so that you will do the best if the worst happens." In practice, however, we rarely behave this way and the minimax can only be defended as a principle of rational behavior in zero-sum games, in which one party wins and the other party loses. Economic life, however, is characterized by non-zero-sum games in which for instance the gain of one party is not necessarily reflected in the loss of another and all parties may gain something. These games can take very complicated forms where what is "rational" is by no means clear. Also game theory can lead to a good deal of mathematical formalism in which the solutions are either incomplete and do not clearly represent the total system or not relevant to problems of real life.

Another important area of mathematics which is relevant to economic problems relates to dynamic theory, which is largely the theory of sequences. Suppose, for instance, that we have a system, the successive states of which in successive "days" are represented by a sequence S_0, S_1, S_2 . . . , S_n. If there is a stable relationship between successive positions in such a sequence, say between S_t and S_{t+1}, then if we are given one state or element in the sequence we can predict all the others. This is what has been called a "difference system," and it is one of the main means by which we can predict the future. If the stable relationship is between two successive states, it is called a system of the first degree. If the stable relationship involves three states, for instance, yesterday, today, and tomorrow, it is a system of the second degree, and so on. Where the state of the system can be expressed by a single number, a difference system may be expressed by a difference equation, which is a functional relationship among successive states of the system. Thus, consider the sequence 100, 105, 110.25, 115.76, 121.55, etc. The difference equation relating any one term S_t to the succeeding term S_{t+1} is $S_{t+1} = 1.05 S_t$. Given this relationship and given an initial value we can project the series as far as we wish. It represents incidentally a sum in the bank growing at 5 percent compound interest. Many economic projections are made by difference systems. Population projections, for instance, are made by difference equations which are based on the fact that every member of a population today will be either one year older or dead this time next year. The projection of trends of all kinds depends on the existence, or rather the assumption, of stable difference systems. The limiting case of a difference equation where the time interval between successive states vanishes toward zero is a differential equation, and most difference systems may be expressed in either form. Most of the beautiful predictions of celestial mechanics, for instance, are obtained by difference systems not exceeding the third degree.

In social systems, and in economic systems in particular, difference systems, while they have a value, must be treated with considerable reserve, as they are almost always subject to unexpected changes in the parameters, that is, in the basic constants of the equations. A good many failures in prediction in the social sciences have followed from shifts of this kind. For instance, during the Second World War most economists were predicting a severe depression within six months after the end of the war, based on the parameters of the system as they had existed in the 1930s. In fact, a severe depression did not occur, mainly because the parameters of the system had changed; after the war people were willing to consume larger proportions of their income than they were in the 1930s, at most levels of income. The population predictions of the mid 1940s, likewise, were completely falsified by the sudden quite unexpected increase in the birthrate in the period that began about 1947 and lasted to well into the 1960s. This "bulge" could hardly have been predicted from earlier data. Here again therefore we have to be careful that we do not let the beauty of mathematical systems run away with us, and while there is a great deal to be said for making projections according to the most sophisticated principles possible, there is also a great deal to be said for not believing them.

Another branch of mathematics which has turned out to be useful in economics is matrix algebra. A matrix is a set of numbers or symbols arranged in a square or rectangular set of boxes or pigeonholes. Matrices can be transformed one into the other through regular algebraic operations in much the same way that numbers can. Matrix algebra is thus a shorthand for what would otherwise be very complicated mathematical or algebraic manipulations. Matrices can also be employed as elements in difference systems. They may be descriptive of successive states of a system, and there may be stable relationships between successive matrices. All this involves in effect an extension of the number concept structures and patterns of numbers.

A number of the features and characteristics of the economic system can conveniently be expressed in matrix form. For instance, we can have an input-output table in which we divide the economy into a number of industries so that each column and each row in the matrix represent a particular segment of the economy. The "box" where a column and a row intersect can then be used to hold a number, let us say the amount the "column" industry puts into the industry represented by the row. A whole matrix of such numbers gives us the inner structure of the economy and shows how the output of each industry is distributed to all the others and the input of each industry is derived from all the others. If the matrix is assumed to have constant coefficients, that is, if the output of each industry is apportioned in the same way among the others, we can do a "sensitivity analysis" for the system and find out what will happen to all the inputs and outputs if one industry is suddenly expanded or contracted.

The amount of mathematics which is actually used in economics represents a relatively small proportion of the total corpus of modern mathematical knowledge. As time goes on, however, and as economists become more educated in the use of mathematics, we may very well find that more erudite branches of mathematics, such as group theory, the theory of numbers, and topology, which might almost be described as the theory of possible shapes, will be brought into use. Their present neglect may be more a matter of the relative unsophistication of economists, even mathematical economists, than of any fundamental inapplicability.

Econometrics and statistics, likewise, are a very important part of the application of mathematics to economics and deserve some mention although we do not have the space for a detailed exposition of their roles. Econometrics might be defined as the science, or perhaps the art, of finding numbers which correspond to the parameters of economic models. The econometrician is not satisfied, for instance, with simply postulating demand and supply functions; he wants to spell them out in detail in the form of explicit equations. He does this by applying various mathematical and statistical techniques to collected data. The direction which econometrics has taken has been very much influenced by the previous existence of general quantitative economic models, such as the models of supply and demand in the determination of prices and the Keynesian models of aggregate national income and its components. It may be indeed that econometrics has been too much influenced by a desire to find numbers for the parameters of preconceived equations. It is quite conceivable that we might go after the matter from the other end and say in effect "here is the observed data spread out through time and space, see what patterns can be perceived in them."

A good deal of effort has been put into econometric studies in the last generation. It must be confessed, however, that the results are a little disappointing. It seems to have been particularly difficult to formulate econometric studies in ways that would lead to the resolution of conflicts between various alternative theories in economics. In monetary theory controversy about the quantity theory of money goes on as briskly now as it did fifty years ago, in spite of the large number of econometric studies that have been done in the interval. Part of the trouble here may be that the development of econometrics has led to a situation in which many of the ablest young minds in the business have been drawn off into the manipulation of data which has been collected by other people for other purposes. With some exceptions there has not been the painstaking attention to the collection of original data which is always necessary if a scientist is to show steady and substantial advance. It may also be that we have not yet directed our empirical work closely enough toward the testing of alternative theories. It may also be that models which rely on smooth well-behaved continuous functions are not constructed to raise some of the more interesting questions in economics, which often concern the precise point at which sharp discontinuities occur. "System-breaks," as I have called them, where one system passes sharply into another and problems, such as the "cliffs" mentioned earlier, appear are among the most interesting phenomena in economics and also perhaps the most important concern of economic policy. One wonders here whether the kind of mathematics which has been most familiar to mathematical economists has not in some degree focused their attention on smoothly operating models and well-behaved functions when the mathematics of discontinuity might have been more appropriate.

Assessing the impact of mathematics on economics, there can be no doubt today that it has been on the whole highly beneficial, and the old controversy, which raged from 1870 to within living memory, as to whether mathematics was appropriate in economics has been resolved firmly in favor of the mathematicians. Nevertheless, economics remains a mixture of mathematics and something that, for want of a better term, we call "not-mathematics." We know pretty well what the mathematics is; it is much harder to define and identify the essential residual element of the subject without which it would not be economics at all but simply a branch of mathematics. The mathematics in economics is strictly applied mathematics. As far as I know, economics has not made a single contribution to pure mathematics, and in no sense is economics a branch of pure mathematics. All the basic mathematical tools which are used in economics were devised by mathematicians and not by economists. If anyone can find a single exception to this rule, I would be most interested and also quite surprised. One is almost tempted to say that mathematics is simply one of the languages in which economics is written. While there is an element of truth in this statement it is also quite misleading, for mathematics, while it is a form of communication, is not a complete language. All mathematical argument, at least all mathematical argument of any length, seems to require connective tissue in the form of a "real" language such as English or German. On the other side of the fence economics may easily have a mathematical content even when it is not expressed in mathematical symbols. The classical economics of Adam Smith and Ricardo is in large part mathematical in the structure of its thought, in the sense that it is concerned with the logical consistency of quantitative relationships, and it is indeed quite easy to translate into mathematics even though it is throughout expressed in standard English. There is mathematical thought even in the most literary of economic writings, and mathematical derivations and chains of reasoning are always subordinate to the economic arguments in any good piece of economics. Indeed it should be the test of good writing in mathematical economics that the reader can skip the mathematical derivations and understand the economic arguments that are being put forward, provided he understands the language of mathematics.

We have still not really identified the "not-mathematics," but perhaps we must attribute this to the immense complexity of its real subject matter, which in large part still defies formal mathematization. To the mathematical economist all commodities tend to look very much alike. They are x's and y's. In the writings of great economists, however, especially those of Adam Smith, there is a sense of the concreteness of commodities—the meatiness of meat, the steeliness of steel, the saltiness of salt, the laboriousness of labor, and even the peculiar pecuniosity of money—as well as of their abstractness. Therefore the economist, as opposed to the pure mathematician, must have an ability to understand that from which he abstracts, as well as the abstraction which must be derived from it. Otherwise, when he tries to apply his model, he may concretize his abstractions in ways which bear no relationship to the real world. Most of all, as we have noted earlier, the economist if he is truly to be a master of his subject must be aware that economics itself abstracts out of the great mass of social life only certain elements and that those things which it does not abstract may be lying in wait down the corner to upset the nice quantitative relationships among his abstractions. By means of mathematics we purchase a great ease of manipulation at the cost of a certain loss of complexity of content. If we ever forget this cost, and it is easy for it to fall to the back of our minds, then the very ease with which we manipulate symbols may be our undoing. All I am saying is that mathematics in any of its applied fields is a wonderful servant but a very bad master; it is so good a servant that there is a tendency for it to become an unjust steward and usurp the master's place. In the training of economists, therefore, it is most desirable that there should be fieldwork in concrete economic situations—in factories, in financial institutions, in labor unions, in governments, and so on—as well as training in the essential skills of mathematical manipulation.

SIX

Economics as a Moral Science[*]

Adam Smith, who has strong claim to being both the Adam and the smith of systematic economics, was a professor of moral philosophy, and it was at that forge that economics was made. Even when I was a student, economics was still part of the moral sciences tripos at Cambridge University. It can claim to be a moral science, therefore, from its origin, if for no other reason. Nevertheless, to many economists the very term "moral science" will seem like a contradiction. We are strongly imbued today with the view that science should be *wertfrei*, and we believe that science has acheived its triumph precisely because it has escaped the swaddling clothes of moral judgment; it has only been able to take off into the vast universe of the "is" by escaping from the treacherous launching pad of the "ought." Even economics, we learn in the history of thought, only became a science by escaping from the casuistry and moralizing of medieval thought. Who, indeed, would want to exchange the delicate rational-

[*] This chapter is adapted from the presidential address delivered to the American Economic Association, Chicago, December 29, 1968, and published in the *American Economic Review*, March, 1969.

ity of the theory of an equilibrium price for the unoperational va-
porings of a "just price" controversy? In the battle between mechanism and moralism generally mechanism has won hands down, and
the very title of this chapter may arouse musty fears of sermonizing
in the minds of many of my readers.

Let me explain first what I mean by moral and moral science. A
moral or ethical proposition is a statement about a rank order of
preference among alternatives which is intended to apply to more
than one person. A preference which applies to one person only is a
"taste." Statements of preferences are often called "value judgments."
If someone says, "I prefer A to B," this is a personal value judgment
or taste. If he says, "A is better than B," there is an implication that
he expects other people also prefer A to B. A moral proposition then
is a "common value."

Every culture, or subculture, is defined by a set of common values,
that is, generally agreed-on preferences. Without a core of common
values a culture cannot exist, and we can classify society into cultures and subcultures precisely because it is possible to identify
groups that have common values.

Most tastes are in fact also common values and have been learned
by the process by which all learning is done, that is, by mutation
and selection. The most absurd of all pieces of ancient wisdom is
surely the Latin tag *de gustibus non disputandum*. In fact, we spend
most of our lives disputing about tastes. If we want to be finicky
about definitions we might turn the old tag around and say where
there is disputing, we are not talking about tastes. Nevertheless, even
personal tastes are learned, in the matrix of the culture or subculture
in which we grow up, by much the same kind of process by which
we learn our common values. Purely personal tastes, indeed, can only
survive in a culture which tolerates them, that is, which has a common value that private tastes of certain kinds should be allowed.

One of the most peculiar illusions of economists is the doctrine of
what might be called the "Immaculate Conception" of the indiffer-

ence curve, that is, the doctrine that tastes are simply given and we cannot inquire into the process by which they are formed. This doctrine is literally "for the birds," whose tastes are largely created for them by their genetic structures and can therefore be treated as a constant in the dynamics of bird societies. In human society, however, the genetic component of tastes is very small indeed. We start off with a liking for milk, warmth, and dryness and a dislike for being hungry, cold, and wet, and we have certain latent drives which may guide the formation of later preferences in matters of sex, occupation, or politics, but by far and away the greater number of human preferences are learned, again by means of a mutation-selection process. It was, incidentally, Veblen's principal, and still largely unrecognized, contribution to formal economic theory to point out that we cannot assume that tastes are given in any dynamic theory, in the sense that in dynamics we cannot afford to neglect the processes by which cultures are created and preferences learned.

I am prepared indeed to go much further and say that no science of any kind can be divorced from ethical considerations, as defined above. The propositions of science are no more immaculately conceived than the preferences of individuals. Science is a human learning process which arises in certain subcultures in human society and not in others, and a subculture as we have seen is a group of people defined by their acceptance of certain common values, that is, an ethic. Without this common ground the extensive interpersonal communication which creates and sustains a subculture is virtually impossible.

The scientific subculture is no exception to this rule. It is characterized by a strong common value system. For instance, a high value is placed on veracity, on curiosity, on measurement, on quantification, on careful observation and experiment, and on objectivity. Without this common value structure the epistemological process of science would not have arisen; indeed it did not arise in certain societies where conditions might otherwise have been favorable but where some essential common values of the scientific subculture did not exist. The question as to exactly what values and ethical propositions are essential to the scientific subculture may be in some dispute. The fact that there are such values cannot be disputed. It is indeed one of the most perplexing questions in intellectual history as to why the scientific subculture developed at the time that it did and why it developed in Western Europe. The common values that are prerequisite to science are rather rare among human subcultures. The common values of political elites, of the military, or of the people who run the international system, to name but a few, are quite different from those of science. In this sense, therefore, science has an essential ethical basis.

This means that even the epistemological content of science, that is, what scientists think they know, has an ethical component. The proposition that water consists of two molecules of hydrogen and one of oxygen is not usually thought of as a proposition with a high ethical content. Nevertheless, any student in chemistry who decides that he prefers to think of hydrogen as dephlogisticated water will soon find out that chemistry is not just a matter of personal taste. The fact that there is no dispute going on about any particular scientific proposition does not mean that its acceptance or rejection is a matter of taste, it simply means that the dispute over its merits has been resolved through the application of certain common values and ethical presuppositions.

There is, however, a fundamental sense in which the epistemological process even in the physical and biological sciences is now running into situations which have strong ethical implications outside the scientific subculture. The notion that science is simply discovering knowledge about an objectively unchangeable world may have had some validity in the early stages of science, but as the sciences have developed it has become less and less valid. The learning process of science is now running into two serious difficulties. The first might be called the generalized Heisenberg principle. According to this principle, when we try to obtain knowledge about a system by changing its inputs and outputs of information, the new inputs and outputs will change the system itself and under some circumstances change it radically. My favorite illustration of the Heisenberg principle is the story of a man who inquires through the door of the bedroom where his friend is sick, "How are you?" whereupon the friend replies, "Fine," and the effort kills him. In the social sciences of course the generalized Heisenberg principle predominates; knowledge of the social sciences is an essential part of the social system itself; hence objectivity in the sense of investigating a world which is unchanged by the investigation of it is an absurdity.

The second difficulty is that as science develops, it no longer merely investigates the world; it creates the world which it is investigating. We see this even in the physical sciences where the evolution of the elements has now been resumed in this part of the universe after some six billion years. We are increasingly going to see this in the biological sciences, which will only find out about the evolutionary process by actively engaging in it and changing its course. In the social sciences one can defend the proposition that almost all we can really know is what we create ourselves and the further proposition that prediction in social systems can be achieved only by setting up consciously created systems which will make the predictions come true. We can obtain knowledge of random systems only by destroying them, that is, by taking the randomness out of them. There is a great deal of evidence, for instance, that the fluctuations of prices in organized commodity or security markets are essentially random in nature, or at least have a very large random component. All we can possibly discover therefore by studying these fluctuations is what bias there might be in the dice. If we want to predict the future of prices in such markets we will have to control them, that is, we will have to set up a system of counterspeculation which will guarantee a given future course of prices. The gold standard is a primitive example of such a system for it is possible to predict that the price of gold will lie within the gold points as long as the system remains intact. Similarly, we can predict the inside temperature of a house with an effective furnace and thermostat much better than we can predict the outside temperature simply because we control one and not the other.

We cannot escape the proposition that as science moves from pure knowledge toward control, that is, toward creating what it knows, what it creates becomes a problem of ethical choice and will depend upon the common values of the society in which the scientific subculture is embedded, as well as the common values of the scientific subculture. Under these circumstances science cannot proceed at all without at least an implicit internal ethic, that is, a subculture with appropriate common values, and it will be destroyed unless the culture in which it is embedded also gives at least minimum support to the scientific ethic. The problem exists in theory even in what might be described as the objective phase of science, that is, the phase in which it is simply investigating "what is," because the question of the conditions under which ignorance is bliss is not an empty one. The assumption, which is almost universal in academic circles, that ignorance cannot possibly be bliss might under some circumstances be proved wrong by the very methods of science itself. As long as science is investigating an unchanging world, however, this problem does not become acute, for if knowledge does not change the world, then all ignorance does for us is to prevent us from satisfying our idle curiosity. When, however, knowledge changes the world, the question of the content of the common values, both of the subculture which is producing knowledge and of the total society in which that subculture is embedded, becomes of acute importance. Under these circumstances the concept of a value-free science is absurd, for the whole future of science may well rest on our ability to resolve the ethical conflicts which the growth of knowledge is now creating. Science *could* create an ethical dynamic which would bring it to an end.

Let us return then to economics as a moral science, not merely in the sense that it like all science is affected with an ethical interest, but in the quite specific sense of asking whether it can be of assistance in resolving ethical disputes, especially those which arise out of the continued increase of knowledge.

Economics specializes in the study of that part of the total social system which is organized through exchange and deals with exchangeables. This to my mind is a better definition of economics than those which define it as relating to scarcity or allocation, for the allocation of scarce resources is a universal problem which applies to political decisions and political structures through coercion, threat and even to love and community, just as it does to exchange. I have elsewhere distinguished three kinds of social organizers which I have called the threat system, the exchange system, and the integrative system. Economics clearly occupies the middle one of these three. It edges over toward the integrative system insofar as it has some jurisdiction over the study of the system of one-way transfers of exchangeables, which I have called the "grants economy," for the grant, or one-way transfer, is a rough measure of an integrative relationship. On the other side, economics edges toward an area between the threat system and the exchange system which might be described as an area of strategy or bargaining.

To complete the circle there is also an area, between the threat system and the integrative system, of legitimated threat, which is the principal organizer of political activity and the main subject matter of political science. All these systems are linked together dynamically through the process of human learning, which is the main dynamic factor in all social systems. Part of this learning process is the learning of common values and moral choices, without which no culture and no social system is possible. The process by which we learn our preference structures indeed is a fundamental key to the total dynamics of society.

Economics, as such, does not contribute very much to the formal study of human learning, though some philosophical economists like Frederick Hayek [1] have made some interesting contributions to this subject. Our main contribution as economists is in the description of what is learned; the preference functions which embody what is learned in regard to values, and the production functions which describe the results of the learning of technology. We may not have thought much about the genetics of knowledge, but we have thought about its description, and this is a contribution not to be despised.

Economists have also thought a great deal about the normative principles of society perhaps because they are the social scientists most interested in the theory of value. We can point to at least three general areas in which economics has made a contribution to general ethical theory. The first is not widely recognized but may be described as a generalization of the theory of exchange value in the direction of ethical and social choice. The second is a large, highly visible body of discussion known as welfare economics. The third, which is practical rather than theoretical, is the impact of economic measurements and indexes upon normative judgments, especially in political life.

Thus, the theory of value in economics suggests the proposition that actual choices depend not only on preferences but on opportunities as well and that under some circumstances quite small changes in either preferences or opportunities may result in large changes in actual choices made, that is, choice may be what we have called a "sensitive" system (page 105). This proposition applies just as much to ethical choices and common values as it does to private tastes. It also throws a good deal of light on what might be called the evolutionary ecology of ethical systems. Successful ethical systems tend to create subcultures, and these subcultures tend to perpetuate and propagate the ethical systems which created them. This principle helps to ex-

[1] F. A. von Hayek, "The Use of Knowledge in Society," *American Economic Review,* 35:519, September, 1945.

plain the persistent division of mankind into sects, nations, and ideo-logical groups. If we were to map the ethical preference systems of the individuals who comprise mankind, we would not find a uni-form distribution, but we would find a very sharp clustering into cultures and subcultures with relatively empty spaces between the clusters. All the members of a single sect, for instance, tend to think rather alike in matters of ethical judgment and to differentiate them-selves sharply from the ethical judgments of other sects. Individuals tend to be attracted to one or another of these clusters, leaving the social space between them relatively empty, like the space between the stars. The reasons for this phenomenon lie deep in the dynamics of the human learning process, for our preferences are learned mainly from those with whom we have the most communication. This principle accounts for the perpetuation of such clusters, though it does not necessarily account for their original formation, which exhibits many puzzling phenomena. The splitting of these clusters in a kind of mitosis is also an important and very puzzling phenome-non. Once we realize, however, that these are highly sensitive sys-tems, as economic analysis suggests, we can see how wide diver-gences might arise. Thus, the actual difference in preferences and even opportunities between, shall we say, the socialist countries and the capitalist countries, may in fact be quite small, but this differ-ence is enough to produce a very wide difference in the choices made. This is a proposition which might easily be overlooked with-out the aid of the techniques of economic analysis.

Next, economics has made a more specific attempt to solve some of the problems involved in moral judgment in what we know as welfare economics. I believe this attempt has been a failure, though a reasonably glorious one, and we should take a brief look at it. Wel-fare economics attempts to answer the question, "What do we mean when we say that one state of a social system is better than another in strictly economic terms?" The most celebrated answer given is the Paretian optimum, which states in effect that condition A of a social system is economically superior to condition B, if nobody feels worse off in A than in B and at least one person feels better off. "Better off" or "worse off" are measured of course by preferences, so we could restate the condition by saying that state A is superior to state B if one or more persons prefer A and nobody prefers B. If we permit internal redistribution within the system, that is, compensation, the range of possible superior states is considerably broadened. From this simple principle a wide range of applications have emerged in a stirring intellectual drama which might well be subtitled "Snow White (the fairest of all) and the Seven Marginal Conditions."

Many, if not most, economists regard the Paretian optimum as almost self-evident. Nevertheless, it rests on an extremely shaky foundation of ethical propositions. The more one examines it, for instance, the more clear it becomes that economists must be extraordinarily nice people even to have thought of such a thing, for it implies that there is no malevolence anywhere in the system. It implies, likewise, that there is no benevolence, the niceness of economists not quite extending as far as goodwill. It assumes selfishness, that is, the independence of individual preference function, such that it makes no difference to me whether I perceive you as better off or worse off. Anything less descriptive of the human condition could hardly be imagined. The plain fact is that our lives are dominated by the very interdependence of utility functions which the Paretian optimum denies. Selfishness, or indifference to the welfare of others, is a knife-edge between benevolence on the one side and malevolence on the other. It is something that is very rare. We may feel indifferent toward those whom we do not know and with whom we have no relationships of any kind, but toward those with whom we have a relationship, even the frigid relationship of exchange, we are apt to be either benevolent or malevolent. We either rejoice when they rejoice, or we rejoice when they mourn.

Economists' almost complete neglect of the concepts of malevolence and benevolence cannot be explained by their inability to handle these concepts with their usual tools. There are no mathematical or conceptual difficulties involved in interrelating utility functions, provided that we note that it is the perceptions that matter.[2] The familiar tools of our trade, the indifference map, the Edgeworth box, and so on, can easily be expanded to include benevolence or malevolence, and indeed without this expansion, many phenomena, such as one-way transfers, cannot be explained. Perhaps the main explanation of our neglect of these concepts lies in the fact that we have concentrated very heavily on exchange as the object of our study, and exchange frequently takes place under conditions of at least relative indifference or selfishness. Nevertheless, there is a minimum degree of benevolence even in exchange; otherwise it cannot be legitimated and operate as a social organizer. We exchange courtesies, smiles, the time of day, and so on with the clerk in the store at the same time that we exchange money for commodities. The amount of benevolence which exchangers feel toward each other need not be large, but a certain minimum is essential. If exchangers begin to feel malevolent toward each other exchange will tend to break down, unless it is legitimated under conditions of special ritual, such as silent trade or collective bargaining.

Nevertheless, economists can perhaps be excused for abstracting from benevolence and malevolence, simply because their peculiar baby, which is exchange, tends to be that social organizer which lies between these two extremes of feeling and produces, if not selfishness at least low levels of malevolence and benevolence. The threat system constantly tends to produce malevolence simply because of the learning process which it engenders. The threatener may begin

[2] K. E. Boulding, "Notes on a Theory of Philanthropy," in Frank Dickinson (ed.), *Philanthropy and Public Policy*, National Bureau of Economic Research, New York, 1962, pp. 57–71.

by feeling benevolent toward the threatened; "I am doing this for your own good," but threats almost invariably tend to make the threatened feel malevolent toward the threatener, and this is likely to produce a type of behavior which will in turn make the threatener feel malevolent toward the threatened. This can easily result in a cumulative process of increasing malevolence which may or may not reach some kind of equilibrium. The breakup of communities into warring factions frequently follows this pattern. At the other end of the scale, the integrative system tends to produce benevolence, and those institutions which are specialized in the integrative system, such as the family, the church, the lodge, the club, the alumni association, and so on, also tend to create and organize benevolence, even beyond the circle of their members. This is partly because benevolence seems to be an important element in establishing a satisfactory sense of personal identity, especially after a threat system has been softened by the development of exchange. Those who live under threat at the lower end of the social scale, as well as those who live by threat at the upper end, tend to find their personal identities either through malevolence and the development of counterthreats or through a process which involves transferring their hatred to weaker objects, such as children and animals. Once this state is passed, however, and society is mainly organized by exchange, there seems to be a strong tendency to move toward an integrative system and integrative institutions. The Rotary Club is a logical extension of a business-oriented society, but it is not one that would necessarily have occurred to economists.

Finally, it is not welfare economics with its elegant casuistry, subtle distinctions, and ultimately rather implausible recommendations which has had the greatest impact on the development of common values and ethical propositions. The major impact of economics on ethics, it can be argued, has come because it has developed broad, aggregative concepts of general welfare which are subject to quantification. We can see this process going right back to Adam Smith.

His idea that what we would today call per capita real income is the principal measure of national well-being, had a profound impact on subsequent thinking and policy. The development of the concept of a gross national product and its various modifications and components that could serve as a statistical measure of economic success, likewise, has been very important in creating common values for the objectives of economic policy. Another, less fortunate, example of a measure which has profoundly affected economic policy is the parity index developed by the Bureau of Agricultural Economics in the U.S. Department of Agriculture. As a measure of the terms of trade of agriculture, this has become an important symbol. "A hundred percent of parity" is the avowed goal of agricultural policy, even though there is very little reason to suppose that the terms of trade of a given historic period, in this case the period 1909 to 1914, have any ultimate validity as an ideal. Because of differing rates of change in productivity in different parts of the economy, we should expect the terms of trade of different sectors to change. If, for instance, productivity in agriculture rises faster than productivity in the rest of the economy, as it has done in the last thirty years, we would expect the terms of trade of agriculture to "worsen" without farmers experiencing any worsening of their incomes or suffering any sense of social injustice.

Even though economic measurement may be abused, its effect on the formation of moral judgments is great and on the whole, I believe, beneficial. For instance, the whole idea of cost-benefit analysis in terms of monetary units, say "real" dollars of constant purchasing power, is of enormous importance in the evaluation of social choices and even of social institutions. We can grant, of course, that the "real" dollar, which oddly enough is a strictly imaginary one, is a dangerously imperfect measure of the quality of human life and human values. Nevertheless, it is a useful first approximation, and when it comes to evaluating difficult choices it is extremely useful to have a first approximation that we can modify. Without some guide line, indeed, all evaluation is random selection by wild hunches. It is true, of course, that cost-benefit analyses, whether of water projects or other pork barrel items or, in more recent years, weapons systems, can be manipulated to suit the prejudices of people who are trying to influence the decisions. Nevertheless, the fundamental principle that we should count all costs, whether easily countable or not, and evaluate all rewards, however hard they are to evaluate, is one which emerges squarely out of economics and one which is at least a preliminary guide line in the formation of moral judgment in what might be called the "economic ethic."

Nevertheless, the economic ethic, or the total cost-benefit principle, is subject to sharp challenge. Two principal criticisms have been made of it, the first of which I think is probably not valid, and the second of which I think may be valid under limited circumstances. The criticism that I think is not valid is that cost-benefit analyses in particular, or economic principles in general, imply a selfish motivation and an insensitivity to the larger issues of malevolence, benevolence, a sense of community, and so on. It is quite true, as shown above, that economists have neglected the problem of malevolence and benevolence. Nevertheless, our attitudes toward others can be measured at least as well as our other preferences, either by some principle of "revealed preference" or by direct questioning. For instance, it is entirely within the competence of economics to develop a "rate of benevolence," defined as the quantity of exchangeables, as measured in real dollars, which a person would be willing to sacrifice in order to contemplate an increase of one real dollar in the welfare of another person. If the rate of benevolence was zero, we, of course, would have indifference or pure selfishness; if the rate of benevolence was negative we would have malevolence, in which case people would need compensation in order to contemplate without loss the increased welfare of an enemy or, in reverse, would be willing to damage themselves in order to damage another. The rate of malevolence then would be the amount in real dollars one would be prepared to damage oneself in order to damage another person to the extent of one dollar. Rates of malevolence incidentally may frequently be quite high. It apparently cost the United States in 1968 about $4 to do $1 worth of damage in Vietnam, which means our rate of malevolence toward North Vietnam was then at least four. In performing a cost-benefit analysis we could easily include rates of benevolence and malevolence, adding the benefits and subtracting the costs of aiding those toward whom we feel benevolent, multiplied of course by the rate of benevolence, and subtracting the benefits and adding the costs, similarly modified, of harming those toward whom we feel malevolent.

Incidentally, the concept of a rate of benevolence is at least a partial solution to the perplexing question of interpersonal comparisons of utility around which economists have been doing a ritual dance for at least three generations. Any decision involving other people obviously involves interpersonal comparisons. They are made, of course, inside the mind of the decision maker, and what his rate of benevolence or malevolence is likely to be is determined by the whole social process in which he is embedded. Surely something can be said about this. We are, for instance, likely to be relatively benevolent to people who are going to vote for us and perhaps malevolent to people who are going to vote against us. The economic theory of democracy, indeed, as developed by Anthony Downs and others, is a very good example of what I have sometimes called "economics imperialism," which is an attempt on the part of economics to take over all the other social sciences.

The second attack on the "economic ethic" is more fundamental and harder to repulse. This is the attack from the side of what I have elsewhere called the "heroic ethic." [3] In facing decisions, especially those which involve other people, as virtually all decisions do, we are faced with two very different frameworks of judgment. The

[3] "Ethical Dilemmas in Religion and Nationalism," lecture at the New York Ethical Society, Apr. 18, 1968.

first of these is the economic ethic of total cost-benefit analysis. It is an ethic of being sensible, rational, respectable, and middle class. It is an ethic of calculation. Indeed we cannot count the cost without counting. Hence, it is an ethic which depends on the development of measures and numbers, even if they are ordinal numbers. This type of decision making, however, does not exhaust the immense complexities of the human organism, and we have to recognize that there is in the world another type of decision making, in which the decision maker elects something, not because of the effects that the decision will have in the future, but because of what he "is" here and now, that is, how he perceives his own identity.

This "heroic" ethic takes three major forms—the military, the religious, and the sporting. The heroic ethic "theirs not to reason why, theirs but to do and die" is so fundamental to the operation of the military that attempts to replace it with an economic ethic in the form of cost-benefit analysis or programmed budgeting or even strategic science as practiced by Herman Kahn, T. C. Schelling, or even Robert McNamara, is deeply threatening to the morale and the legitimacy of the whole military system. Religion, likewise, is an essentially heroic enterprise, even though there is a strong streak of spiritual cost-benefit analysis in some of its manifestations. The enormous role which religion has played in the history of mankind, for good or ill, is based on the appeal which it has to the sense of identity and the sense of the heroic even in ordinary people. "Here I stand and I can do no other," said Luther; "To give and not to count the cost, to labor and ask for no reward" is the prayer of Saint Francis. "Do your own thing" is the motto of our new secular Franciscans, the hippies. In our national religion, President Kennedy said, "Ask not what your country can do for you, ask only what you can do for your country." We find the same principle in poetry and art and architecture, which are constantly striving to disengage themselves from the chilling embrace of cost-benefit analysis. I cannot resist quoting here in full what has always seemed to me one of the finest expressions in English poetry of the heroic critique of economics—Wordsworth's extraordinary sonnet on King's College Chapel, Cambridge (Ecclesiastical Sonnet, Number XLIII).

INSIDE OF KING'S COLLEGE CHAPEL, CAMBRIDGE

Tax not the royal Saint with vain expense,
With ill-matched aims the Architect who planned—
Albeit labouring for a scanty band
Of white-robed Scholars only—this immense
And glorious Work of fine intelligence!
Give all thou canst; high Heaven rejects the lore
Of nicely-calculated less or more;
So deemed the man who fashioned for the sense
These lofty pillars, spread that branching roof
Self-poised, and scooped into ten thousand cells,
Where light and shade repose, where music dwells
Lingering—and wandering on as loth to die;
Like thoughts whose very sweetness yieldeth proof
That they were born for immortality.

Okay, boys, bring out your cost-benefit analysis now. There is a story, for the truth of which I will not vouch, that Keynes once asked the chaplain of King's College if he could borrow the chapel for a few days. The chaplain was overjoyed at this evidence of conversion of a noted infidel until it turned out that Keynes had got caught short with a load of wheat in the course of his speculations in futures and wanted to use the chapel for storage.

The "lore of nicely calculated less or more," of course, is economics. I used to think that high heaven rejected this because its resources were infinite and therefore did not need to be economized. I have since come to regard this view as unsound not only for theological reasons which I cannot go into here, but also for a more fundamental reason. High heaven, at least as it exists and propagates itself in the minds of men, is nothing if not heroic. The power of religion in human history has arisen primarily from its capacity to give identity to its practitioners and inspire them to behave in accordance with this perceived identity. In extreme form, this gives rise to saints and martyrs of all faiths, religious or secular, but it also gives rise to a great deal of quiet heroism, for instance, in jobs, in marriage, in child rearing, and in the humdrum tasks of daily life, without which a good deal of the economy might well fall apart.

A good deal of the criticism of economics from both left and right arises from dissatisfaction with its implied neglect of the heroic. There is a widespread feeling that trade is somehow dirty, merchants are somewhat undesirable characters, and the labor market is utterly despicable as constituting the application of the principle of prostitution to virtually all areas of human life. This sentiment is not something which economists can neglect. We have assumed all too easily in economics that because something paid off it was automatically legitimate. Unfortunately, the dynamics of legitimacy are more complex than this. Frequently it is negative payoffs, that is, sacrifices, rather than positive payoffs, which establish legitimacy. It has been the precise weakness of the institutions that we think of as primarily economic, that is, associated with exchange, such as the stock market, the banking system, organized commodity markets, and so on, that, as Schumpeter pointed out, they easily lose their legitimacy if they are not supported by other elements and institutions in society which can sustain them as integral parts of a larger community. On the right also we find nationalists, fascists, and the military attacking the economic man and economic motivation from the point of view of the heroic ethic. It is a wonder indeed that economic institutions can survive at all, when the economic man is so universally unpopular. No one in his senses would want his daughter to marry an economic man, one who counted every cost and asked for every reward, was never afflicted with mad generosity or uncalculating love, and who never acted out of a sense of inner identity and indeed had no inner identity even if he was occasionally affected by carefully calculated considerations of benevolence or malevolence. The attack on economics is an attack on calculatedness, and the very fact that we think of the calculating as cold suggests how exposed economists are to romantic and heroic criticism.

My personal view is that, especially at his present stage of development, man requires both heroic and economic elements in his institutions, in his learning processes, and in his decision making, and the problem of maintaining them in proper balance and tension is one of the major problems of maturation, both of the individual person and of societies. Economic man is a clod, heroic man is a fool, but somewhere between the clod and the fool, human man, if the expression may be pardoned, steers his tottering way.

Let me conclude by stealing yet another idea from economics and applying it to general moral science. This is the concept of a production function, some sort of limited relationship between inputs and outputs as expressed in the great Biblical principle that grapes are not gathered from thorns, or figs from thistles (Matthew 7:16). There are production functions not only for grapes and figs but also for goods and bads, and indeed for the ultimate Good. We dispute about what is good, about what outputs we want as a result of the inputs we put in; we dispute also however about the nature of the production functions themselves, that is, about what inputs will in fact produce what outputs. In the case of physical production functions the problems can be resolved fairly easily by experimenting, even though there are some pretty doubtful cases, as in the case of cloud seedings, which do not seem to be demonstrably more certain in their effect than rain dances. In the case of moral production functions, however, the functions themselves are much in dispute; indeed there may be more disputation about the production functions than there is about the nature of the desired outputs themselves. I was impressed some years ago, when engaged in a long, arduous seminar with some young Russians and young Americans, with how easy it was to agree on ultimate goals, even across these widely divergent ideologies, and how extraordinarily hard it was to agree about the inputs which are likely to lead to these ultimate goals.

There is a problem here in human learning of how we get to know the moral production functions in the complex melée of social, political, and economic life, when it seems to be pervaded throughout with a note of almost cosmic irony in which almost everything we do turns out different from what we expect because of our ignorance, so that both the bad and the good we do is all too often unintentional. I cannot solve this epistemological problem in one short essay, but I recommend it as a major intellectual challenge to the moral sciences. What I am concerned with here is with economics as an input into this moral production function. Does economics, as George Stigler has suggested,[4] make people conservative? If so, perhaps it is because it simply points out the difficulties and dangers of heroic action and makes people appreciate the productivity of the commonplace, of exchange and finance, of bankers and businessmen, and even of the middle class which our heroic young so earnestly despise. Perhaps this is why so many young radicals today have treated economics as a poisoned apple of rationality which corrupts the pure and heroic man of their identities and sympathies. Economics is a reconciler, it brings together the ideologies of East and West, it points up the many common problems which they have, it is corrosive of ideologies and disputes that are not worth their costs. Even as it acts as a reconciler, however, does it not undermine that heroic demand for social mutation which will not be stilled in the voices of our young radicals?

On the other hand, when we turn to what might be called the "Marxist mutation" we find something which looks like economics and yet is clearly heroic rather than economic in its ethical values. Who would have thought indeed that the dry abstractions of the Ri-

[4] G. J. Stigler, "The Politics of Political Economists," *Quarterly Journal of Economics,* 73:522, November, 1959.

cardian theory of value could have been formed into a trumpet of revolution! In the cost-benefit analysis of the ultimate recording angel Marxism may well turn out to have done more harm than good, and even if its heroic qualities and its capacity to inspire large masses of men for good or ill are derived from Hegel rather than Ricardo, it is hard to remove the stamp of economics from an economic interpretation of history! Marxist heroics, however, have created an enormous debit account that includes not only bloodshed but also the corruption of simple human relationships, the suppression of creativity and the arts, and of the kind of monstrous political paranoia that one saw in Stalin and one sees today in Mao Tse Tung. Perhaps then economics must be condemned more on the side of inspiring heroic stupidity than on the side of inculcating a cold calculatedness.

I confess I have been deeply disturbed when I have asked myself these questions, and I have no easy answers to them. Nevertheless, I am not sorry that I became an economist, for to belong to a body of people who have never even thought of introducing malevolence into their social theory is somehow in this day and age a little cheering.

The American Economic Association in 1968, the year in which I was its president, was racked by a passionate dispute which had many facets but was symbolized by the question whether we should move the annual meetings scheduled for December, 1968 in Chicago away from that city as a protest against the events and the policies which had surrounded the Democratic National Convention in Chicago that summer. A moral cost-benefit analysis applied to the problem suggested that the benefits of a protest move were very dubious and the costs were very real. Nevertheless, the need for a heroic gesture of protest was felt so strongly and by so many people that the Association was threatened with a split. Strangely enough it was the econometricians who were most heroically moved by the sense of outrage against their personal identity and who were least affected by cost-benefit analysis and who, therefore, moved their meetings at great inconvenience to themselves to the purer and drier satellite city of Evanston. It is clear, therefore, that the study of economics, even in its most austere forms, does not produce clods, as even economists are capable of mild heroics. We can have some hope, therefore, that economics is one of the inputs that help to make us human. If so, the benefits of this strange activity will be well worth its undoubted cost, even if in our heroic mood we dare not calculate them.

SEVEN

Economics and the Future of Man

In these chapters I have taken the view that economics is primarily the study of how society is organized through exchange, extending this to the grants economy through the one-way transfer of exchangeables. I have argued that the problems of scarcity and allocation are not peculiar to economics but are problems of the general social system and of all the social sciences and that exchange is not the only instrument by which the allocation of scarce resources takes place. Nevertheless, the scarcity of exchangeables does seem to be the peculiar province of economics, and it is the scarcity of exchangeables which creates what we usually think of as economic activity. Furthermore, exchangeables, with the exception of money and other things which may be used as means of exchange, are exchangeables precisely because they are also something else, because they are objects which meet the needs and desires of man. This is the aspect of economics which might be called "provisioning," the providing of those things which need to be provided if human life is to be secure, comfortable, happy, adventurous, dangerous, heroic, and whatever else we may want it to be. In the past, I have poked a little fun at the kind of view of economics which regards its focus as primarily that of provisioning by calling it "Pooh-Bear" economics. All those who have used their children as an excuse to read A. A. Milne will recall that Pooh never went on an "expotion" without a heavy investment in Provisions, which mostly consisted of honey.[1] Nevertheless, the view that economics is concerned with provisioning rather than with exchange is probably closer to the popular view of what economics is all about than is the more abstract view which I have been propounding in this volume.

We can perhaps achieve a partial resolution of this dilemma by distinguishing between economic science in a narrow sense, which I would maintain is the study of how society is organized through exchange and through transfers of exchangeables, and what might be called the economic problem, which is really the problem of provisioning, providing the good things of life. Most provisions indeed are exchangeables but not all, so that provisioning as a general problem includes not only the provisioning of food, clothing, shelter, travel, personal services, and all the things which participate in the exchange system, but also the provisioning of security from threat and violence, status and dignity, civil rights, social justice, equal status with others as a person, and other things which we think of as part of the political and sociological aspects of life rather than economic. At the intersection of these two sets we get the concept of economics as that science which studies the provisioning of exchangeables. This makes economics relevant to the welfare of man and prevents it from falling into the trap of being an irrelevant abstract theory of exchange, the study indeed of the no-person group. The definition also points up the fact, however, that the provisioning of exchangeables is done mainly through the mechanism of exchange and can only be understood by understanding that mechanism.

[1] See especially my review of Adolph Lowe, *On Economic Knowledge:* "Is Economics Obsolescent?" *Scientific American,* 212(5):139–143, May, 1965.

A question which is constantly asked of economists these days is whether the development of a technologically created abundance has not destroyed economics altogether and made it obsolete. One finds this view particularly on the vaguely anarchistic left, but it is also present in the writings of men like Robert Theobald.[2] Even in the general field of discussion of liberal church people this view has received wide currency. There is widespread fear, for instance, that the development of automation will create enormous unemployment, and a great deal of popular literature propounds the view that the onset of universal abundance is going to force us to make drastic changes in an economic system which everybody knows was designed to deal with the problem of scarcity.

Not even economists themselves have been altogether immune to the beatific vision of the abolition of economics. J. M. Keynes envisioned a future in which affluence would become so general that economics would become relatively unimportant.

> I draw the conclusion that, assuming no important wars and no important increase in population, the *economic* problem may be solved, or be at least within sight of solution, within a hundred years. This means that the economic problem is not—if we look into the future—*the permanent problem of the human race.*[3]

Karl Marx envisioned a world

> where each one does not have a circumscribed sphere of activity but can train himself in any branch he chooses; society by regulating the common production makes it possible for me to do this today and that tomorrow, to hunt in the morning, to fish in the afternoon, to carry on cattle-breeding in

[2] Robert Theobald, *The Rich and the Poor; A Study of the Economics of Rising Expectations*, Potter, New York, 1960 and *Free Men and Free Markets*, Anchor Books, Garden City, N.Y., 1965.

[3] J. M. Keynes, *Essays in Persuasion*, Norton, New York, The Norton Library, 1963, pp. 365–366.

> the evening, also to criticize the food—just as I please—without becoming either hunter, fisherman, shepherd or critic.[4]

The classical economists of course were not so sanguine. They did visualize development towards a stationary state, but at its best, it would be, as Adam Smith said, "dull," and at its worst, in the Malthusian vision, it would be horrible, with starvation and misery limiting a hopelessly overcrowded population and a small class of luxurious landlords consuming whatever surplus there might be. The apostles of abundance, of course, may dismiss this as appropriate merely to the early stages of technological development, which science has now made wholly obsolete.

It is my considered view that these projections of the developmental process into a society of effortless abundance in which economics, like the state, has withered away are fantasies arising from a rather naïve extrapolation of what may eventually be seen historically as a rather brief period in the history of man. It is true, of course, that for the last two hundred years man, especially in the temperate zones of the world, has been getting very much richer than he was before, as measured by per capita real income. His provisions have increased in quantity and variety to the point where the scale of human life by comparison with anything that has gone before has become reasonably ample in regard to such provisions as food, clothing, shelter, information inputs, and travel. This is true for about a third of mankind; two-thirds of the human race remain in the condition of severely limiting poverty in which man has lived for most of his history.

There is little doubt that short of catastrophe this process of development will continue and expand to more and more people. Nevertheless, it is a process which will not go on indefinitely. One nonexistence theorem, as the mathematicians say, about the universe is

[4] Karl Marx, *Capital and Other Writings,* Modern Library, New York, 1932, p. 1.

that growth at a constant rate cannot go on forever, or even for very long. Otherwise, there would soon be only one thing in the universe. Every growth curve exhibits a declining rate of growth as the thing that is growing increases in size. We see this in all living organisms; they have a high rate of growth in youth which falls to zero in adulthood and becomes negative in old age. Social organizations and structures eventually follow the same pattern, even though their growth curves are usually not simple but consist of successive periods of rising or falling rates of growth. Eventually, however, the growth of any particular growing structure must come to an end. The economic growth which has been characteristic of the last two hundred years is no exception to this rule. It is not a process which will proceed indefinitely into the future at existing rates. There is a great deal of evidence that it is already slowing down; indeed there is evidence that the growth of the per capita gross national product in those countries which are following the course of successful development is declining as the per capita gross national product itself increases.

Figure 7-1, in which the rate of growth of per capita gross national product is plotted against the per capita gross national product itself for as many countries as figures are available, tells us a great deal about the present state of the world. We see, for instance, that the countries of the world divide themselves pretty sharply into two groups. One group which may be called Group A, consists mostly of countries in the temperate zone. It represents what I would call the "main line" of development. We see clearly that for this group of countries the rate of growth is correlated inversely with the gross national product per capita, which is a measure of how rich they are already. These countries, therefore, follow the principle of the richer, the slower. The second group of countries, which I have called Group B, exhibits virtually no correlation at all between the rate of growth and per capita GNP, suggesting that growth here is a fairly random process and there is no main line of development

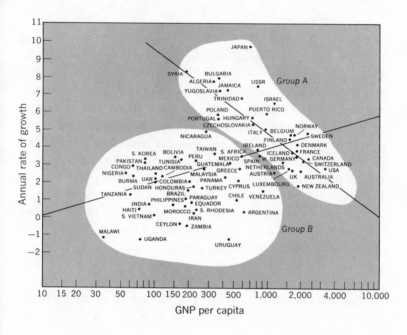

FIGURE 7-1

as yet. These countries are mostly in the tropics, though Chile, Argentina, and Uruguay are depressing examples of countries which unquestionably were on the main line of development at one time, but fell off it as a result of political mismanagement. This shows, indeed, that development is by no means an automatic process and that it is perfectly possible for countries to "take off" and then fall back on the launching pad.

The "main line" which shows the relationship between the rate of growth and the GNP per capita for the Group A countries cuts the zero rate of growth line at about $10,000 per capita. If, therefore, we project the per capita GNP of the successful countries for the next two hundred years we get a figure very much like Figure 7-2, which shows that if the parameters which are characteristic of the system

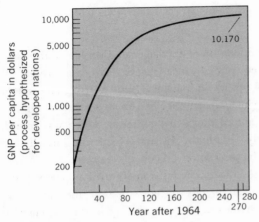

FIGURE 7-2

in the 1960s persist, the rate of growth will slow down very appreciably in another hundred years and virtually come to an end in two hundred. We should not, of course, take these projections too seriously for they can always be falsified by changes in the growth process itself. There is some evidence, indeed, that the growth process is changing. If we repeat this analysis for the 1950s, for instance, we find that the gross national product per capita at which the rate of growth becomes zero is about $5,000 rather than $10,000, which suggests that the growth process itself has been somewhat different in the 1960s from what it was in the 1950s.

Figure 7-1, incidentally, shows how dangerous correlation analysis can be if it is applied mechanically, as it is all too often. If we do a correlation for all the countries we find that growth actually increases with an increase in per capita GNP. This, however, is pure statistical illusion arising out of the fact that we are aggregating two essentially different systems. It is one of the dangers of the enormous expansion of computing power which has come with the development of the electronic computer that it has reduced the contact of the investigator with the data and hence has increased his power to

produce nonsense as well as his power to discover more intricate relationships.

There are considerations more fundamental than the rather mechanical ones outlined above which suggest that the process of
human expansion will not go on indefinitely and that we face indeed
a major crisis ahead which we may not be able to surmount. The nature of the crisis is summed up in the expression which was coined,
I think independently, by both Barbara Ward and myself—the
"Spaceship Earth." [5] In the last few thousand years the human race
has been expanding almost continuously in its total population and
in what might be called its rate of utilization of the earth's resources. This process has accelerated enormously in the last hundred
years. Up to the present time man has lived in the "era of the great
plane" in which his image of the world has been essentially that of a
flat earth on which he could expand indefinitely with new lands and
new resources always somewhere over the horizon. Today the era of
geographical expansion has come to an end—there are no empty
lands, and the view of earth from space dramatizes the image of man
as inhabiting a small, closed spaceship, destination unknown and resources limited.

For the last two hundred years the discovery of new resources and
improved means of utilization of old resources through the advance
of knowledge has proceeded faster than the expansion of population,
at least in the successfully developing parts of the world. We are beginning to face the fact, however, that the kind of "linear economy,"
which is peculiarly characteristic of modern technology, which ex-
tracts fossil fuels and ores at one end and transforms them into commodities and ultimately into waste products which are spewed out
the other end into pollutable reservoirs is a process which is inher-

[5] B. Ward Johnson, *Spaceship Earth*, Columbia, New York, 1966;
K. E. Boulding, "The Economics of the Coming Space-Ship Earth,"
in Henry Jarrett (ed.), *Environmental Quality in a Growing Economy, Essays from the Sixth RFF Forum*, Johns Hopkins for Resources
for the Future, Inc., Baltimore, 1966, pp. 3–14.

ently suicidal and must eventually come to an end, either through the exhaustion of the resources in the mines and wells at the one end or through the exhaustion of the "sinks," that is, pollutable reservoirs, at the other end. The end of this spectacular process of development through which we are going indeed could easily be a virtually dead earth with all its concentration of ores and energy sources depleted and all its pollutable reservoirs filled up.

Therefore, if the society toward which we are developing is not to be a nightmare of exhaustion, we must use the interlude of the present era to develop a new technology which is based on a circular flow of materials such that the only source of man's provisions will be his own waste products. In a spaceship there are neither mines nor sewers, and man has to find a place for himself provisioned by a circular flow of materials which happens to take a form unusually favorable to him in the place that he happens to occupy. There is no way, of course, thanks to the dismal second law of thermodynamics, that a circular system of this kind can be achieved without inputs of energy. From the human point of view, fortunately, the energy input from the sun can be regarded as virtually inexhaustible, as when that goes the evolutionary process, in this part of the universe at least, is presumably over. All known earthly sources of energy, even uranium, will be exhausted quite rapidly if development continues to accelerate. The possible exception to this is the use of nuclear fusion as an earthly source of energy. The problems which this presents, however, are almost as great as those presented to the man who was looking for the universal solvent when somebody asked him what he would keep it in.

Whatever the technology of the spaceship earth it is clear that economics will not disappear. Indeed scarcity may be more omnipresent than it is in our wildly extravagant and expansive world of today. One could certainly visualize a technology that would provide the basic necessities for physical health and comfort for all. There is, however, an ineradicable scarcity of land, especially of agreeable environments. We already seem to be within sight of an era when the main condition differentiating the rich and the poor will be access to sheer physical space. In matters of food, clothing, warmth, medical care, and so on, one would expect that in the next fifty years in the developed countries the poor will not fare very much worse than the rich. What the poor will not have, however, is space around them. The labor theory of value originated at a time when the principal source of the scarcity of commodities was the fact that each man only had twenty-four hours a day to spend, of which usually not much more than twelve could be spent in producing commodities. Where the productivity of labor is low, the amount of labor embodied in a commodity may be the principal factor limiting its output and thereby creating value. As labor becomes more productive it may well be that relative prices will depend more on land input than on labor input, despite land-saving improvements, such as the increased yield of crops or the building of skyscrapers. However we look at it, it is virtually impossible to visualize a world in which scarcity has really come to an end, that is, a world in which everybody is satiated with provisions of all kinds.

This is not to say, of course, that the economic system of spaceship earth may not look very different from the economic systems of today, whether capitalist or communist. Oddly enough, the traditional village economy, especially of Asia, may be more a prototype of the world to come than the economies of the great age of expansion in which we are now living, for to a considerable extent the village was cyclical, did return all waste products to the earth, and did not depend very much on imports from outside. It, of course, was a low-level cyclic economy from which we have gratefully escaped. Nevertheless, what we are looking for in the spaceship is a high level cyclical economy, some of the features of which may have been foreshadowed in the traditional village.

A very interesting question to which I do not know the answer is what will be the nature of social and economic organization in the spaceship earth. Will it have to be, for instance, a tightly, centrally planned society organized along authoritarian lines, such as we have in the communist states, or will it be a looser, free-market type of economy, using the price system as a motivator for change, where change is necessary, within a sufficient framework of generally accepted principles and authority to insure long-run stability. It is quite possible that both patterns will be feasible. To my own way of thinking, the second would be much to be preferred. A system with private property, a wide freedom of choice of location and occupation, a variety of subcultures and the possibility of moving from one to the other, the kind of things in short that we think of today as characterizing a free society is by no means necessarily incompatible with a spaceship, providing that certain overall, main variables of the system are under social, even automatic control.

There must, for instance, be stability of population or at least a rate of increase which is commensurate with any increase in the carrying capacity of the spaceship. This could be achieved, as I have suggested earlier,[6] through a market mechanism which I have sometimes called my Green Stamp Plan for population control, according to which each human being would receive in adolescence, say, 110 green stamps, 100 of which would entitle the owner to have one legal child. A market would then be set up in these instruments so that those who had a strong desire for children could buy stamps from those who did not want to have children. Individual preferences in this matter could thus be expressed, while at the same time society could maintain overall social control of the rate of growth of population. There would presumably have to be mild sanctions for having illegal children which might entail temporary sterilization until the illegal children are paid for in green stamps. This scheme has met with a good deal of disapproval. The alternative, however, would surely be authoritarian control with a set number of children al-

[6] K. E. Boulding, *The Meaning of the Twentieth Century*, Harper & Row, New York, 1965.

lowed per family and severe sanctions for violating the allotted number.

I use the above plan merely as an illustration of how overall social control of the kind which will be required in the spaceship may be achieved through a market mechanism with the least interference with individual liberty and differentiation of personality and culture. We might well be able to work out similar institutions for the resolution of conflicts, which will be another acute problem in the spaceship. War may be tolerable on the great plane, but it simply will not do in the close confines of the spaceship, and we must devise better methods of conflict resolution than we now have or we will simply not survive as a developed society. I have some hope, therefore, that while the spaceship earth may feel tight and uncomfortable by comparison with the wild freedom of the age of expansion in which we now live, human ingenuity can make it tolerable. It may be indeed that our descendants will regard us as the lucky occupants of a time of exciting transition and look back on our time with much the same nostalgia as we look back on the time of cowboys and Indians. One hopes, however, that it will be a mild nostalgia and that the overall quality of human life will be much higher in the developed society to come than it is now. I have sometimes characterized the whole age of civilization in which we have been living and which is now passing away as a rather deplorable interlude in the state of man characterized by exploitation, war, poverty, large-scale misery, and slavery, as well as by occasional peaks of artistic achievement, a period which lies between the "Eden" of the neolithic, when the lot of the average man apparently was better than it has been under civilization, and hopefully the "Zion" to come in the developed society, when war and exploitation will vanish from the earth.

In the light of this kind of image of the future one might return to economics as it is practiced by economists today, and ask what kind of contribution are we making toward the successful handling of the enormous and precarious transition through which mankind is passing. The answer is fairly clear that we are making some contribution, enough indeed to have established us as the most successful of the scientists, at least as judged by our political influence through such things as the Council of Economic Advisers and the Joint Economic Committee in Congress and the mundane fact that our salaries are the highest of all the academic professions, exceeding even those of physicists. Our success has come in two fields: one in macro economics and employment policy and the other in the field of the analysis of economic behavior and the improvement of the information systems of powerful decision makers by such things as linear programming, program budgeting, and even game theory. Our success in the first field can be visualized very easily if we simply contrast the twenty years after the First World War, in which we had the Great Depression and an international situation which ended in Hitler and the disaster of the Second World War, with the twenty years after the Second World War, in which we had no Great Depression, merely a few little ones, and the United States had the longest period of sustained high employment and growth in its history. In spite of Vietnam we are certainly further from World War III in 1969 than we were from World War II in the corresponding year of the first period, which would be 1945! Not all of this is due to economics, but some of it is, and even if only a small part of it is, the rate of return on the investment in economics must be enormous. The investment has really been very small and the returns, if we measure them by the cost of the depressions which we have not had, could easily run into a trillion dollars. On quite reasonable assumptions, therefore, the rate of return on economics has been on the order of tens of thousands of percent in the period since the end of World War II. It is no wonder that we find economists at the top of the salary scale!

Our achievements in the improvement of economic decision making are perhaps harder to evaluate. One could argue indeed that economics has had certain negative effects in that it has improved efficiency in the doing of things that probably should not be done at all. This is the problem of "suboptimization," which I have been arguing is one of the real names of the devil, as it is a source of so much human misery. An increase in the efficiency with which we produce what from our point of view of society are negative goods is by no means to be desired. Oddly enough, it is only economics out of all the social sciences that has thought much about this problem or has come up with any solution to it. This, indeed, is the classical problem of the "invisible hand," that is, what are the circumstances under which everybody doing what is best for himself also produces what is best for society. The economists' solution of perfect markets for everything, unfortunately, is impractical in practice, for two reasons. First, there is a strong consumer demand for heterogeneity in commodities. We do not like standardized items, and we do like a great variety of choice. Under these circumstances the number of different commodities offered for sale tends to multiply with the result that the market for each particular commodity is restricted and becomes imperfect. The other reason why perfect competition is impossible is that in a number of areas of economic life there are economies of scale that accrue to very large-scale organizations such as we see in telephones, automobiles, and all the so-called public utilities. Nevertheless, the problem of how to simulate something like perfect markets remains as an unsolved problem of political and social organization, and the economic solution, unacceptable as it may be, is at least a place to start.

In spite of the successes of economics, it has also had two rather conspicuous failures. I would suggest that its first major failure, in the last generation, has been its failure to develop an adequate theory of economic development and to come up with an adequate set of policy recommendations for the poor countries who are not on the "main line" of development, in spite of the large amount of attention paid to this subject. Figure 7-1 shows very clearly the division of the world into the successfully developing countries of Group A and the unsuccessful ones of Group B. The figures themselves should not be taken too literally, especially in the case of the poor countries, as national income statistics leave a great deal to be desired, but improvement of the data, while it will change the status of a few particular countries, is not likely to change the overall pattern. The failure to provide poor countries with helpful advice is, I suspect, the result of the fact that economists have worked too narrowly within the confines of their own abstractions and their own discipline and have not recognized that a development process is something which involves the total society and that hence purely economic models have a very limited value. The study of development as a total dynamic pattern of social life is one that requires full cooperation between different social scientists and this has not really been forthcoming.

The second failure of economics is in the field of urban poverty and deterioration and the whole matter of the provision of a decent physical environment. The defect here I suspect is more a failure to allocate intellectual resources properly within the economics profession than it is a failure to integrate with other social scientists, although in such matters as the self-perpetuation of poverty subcultures economists have a great deal to learn from social anthropologists. The plain fact is that even when it comes to urban economics, within the narrow framework of such problems as real estate, land speculation, transportation, and tax systems, which are clearly within the general purview of the discipline of economics, we find a serious lack not only of theory but, more importantly, of data. What might be called the economic dynamics or the economic ecology of the city is something that has been given shockingly little attention. Partly this is a result of the accident of the organization of the educational system. Because of the Morrill Act of 1862 and the setting up of land-grant colleges, the agricultural industry quite early developed excellent contacts with all the sciences. As a result of this institutional arrangement, agricultural economics has been blessed with a great deal of money and has developed to the point where the effort which goes into it is far out of proportion to the quantitative importance of the agricultural sector of the economy. We did not develop similar universities for architecture and the building trades. As a result, architecture has remained in a "fine arts" environment with poor contacts even with the physical sciences and virtually no contacts with the social sciences. The building trades have remained a bastion of folk technology and small-scale organization, putting virtually nothing into research and keeping isolated from the onrush of science-based technology. Given the combination of weak municipal governments, municipal tax systems which discourage improvements, transportation systems which are destructive of amenity, architects who cater almost entirely to the foibles of the rich, and a building industry which has just barely emerged from the middle ages, it is hardly surprising that our cities are in decay. A major intellectual effort to plot their revival, in which economists should play an important role, is clearly indicated.

A related area which economists have neglected, again perhaps because there has been no real social organization which has provided a niche for these kinds of studies, is the study of the economics of threats, violence, crime, police, and the armed forces. This is an area which has been of increasing importance unfortunately in the last generation. For instance the proportion of the gross national product going into national defense has risen from about 1 percent in 1930 to nearly 10 per cent today. This is a very major structural change, yet it has been surprisingly little studied by economists. The economics of police and crime is practically an unknown field. It is about as little developed as the economics of the building industry.

An area where there has been a great deal of effort on the part of economists, with I suspect inadequate productivity, is in the field of money, banking, and finance, which is traditionally the most "economic" of all fields in the social sciences. Perhaps, however, its economic status is just what is the matter with it. Economists have studied the behavior of innumerable time series and the patterns of revealed data; hardly anybody has studied the actual decision-making processes of financial organizations and especially the processes by which these organizations determine the flow of information and information inputs which determines their decisions. There is a whole area here which might be called the economic sociology of the market. It hardly exists as a field of study, yet I suspect it contains most of the answers to the questions about the financial system which still seem to be unresolved after thirty or more years of hard empirical study of purely financial data on the part of economists.

I would not wish to disparage the great achievements of mathematical economics and econometrics in the last generation in the matter of the development of techniques for the analysis of strictly economic data. Nevertheless, I cannot help wondering whether this is not an effort that is now running into diminishing returns in the sense that it has exploited pretty fully the kind of data which is readily available and is now producing more and more analyses and less and less information. This judgment does not necessarily apply to the quantitative analysis of historical data from the past, especially the more remote past, which has produced some extremely interesting results and is certainly revising our image of human history. Nevertheless, just as no stream can rise above its source, no science can rise above its original data collection, and one would like to see a revival of interest in economics in the improved collection of raw data, especially at the levels of individual and organizational behavior.

Here again one does not want to disparage the very important work which has been done by such organizations as the Survey Research Center at the University of Michigan and similar organizations elsewhere in improving the collection of original data. On the whole, however, the quick returns in economics in the last thirty years have been through bright young mathematically inclined economists who have devoted themselves to the analysis of existing data rather than to the collection of new data at the source. Our training methods in graduate schools have accentuated this tendency to the point where we now perhaps have actually retrogressed in the training of people who are skilled in finding out what the real world is like.

It is a sad commentary on the American scene in economics that the only really indigenous American school of economists, the institutionalists, represented for instance by John R. Commons at Wisconsin, left only a handful of descendants. I would not be surprised if the majority of graduate students studying economics in American universities do not even know the names of the great American empiricists and institutionalists of the past. It is fashionable indeed to decry the history of thought as a luxury in these days of econometrics, to proclaim that it is of no greater significance than, shall we say, the history of mathematics. This attitude it seems to me is disastrous, for it limits the graduate student to the fashions of the present and easily leads him into a tight little intellectual box from which there is no escape. The successes of economics should not blind us to the fact that its subject matter is a system far more complex than the systems which are studied by the natural scientists, for instance, and we must recognize that our most elegant models can be no more than the crudest of first approximations of the complex reality of the systems which they purport to represent. If we educate out of our students that almost bodily sense of what the real world is like even though we may see it through a glass darkly, a trait which was so characteristic of the great economists of the past, something of supreme value will be lost. Our graduate schools may easily be producing a good deal of the "trained incapacity" which Veblen saw being produced in his day, and this is a negative commodity unfortunately with a very high price.

Nevertheless, whatever happens to economics the problems will remain and as long as the problems remain, men will be impelled to study them. If the formal study of economics boxes itself in so much that real economics problems will have to be studied outside it, this will be worse for economics than it is for mankind. One hopes, however, that economists will perceive the trap that may lie ahead of them and will play their full part as a profession in the management of the great transition which lies ahead of us.